Suffolk Enterprise:

A Guide to the County's Companies and their Historical Records

Christine Clark & Roger Munting

Centre of East Anglian Studies

©Christine Clark and Roger Munting

ISBN 0-906219-51-5

All rights reserved. No part of this publication may be reproduced, stored in a retrieval system or transmitted, in any form or by any means, electronic, mechanical or otherwise, without permission of the Author.

Published by the University of East Anglia, Norwich NR4 7TJ

Printed by The Print Group at the University of East Anglia

Design by PK back:up, Norwich

Contents

List of illustrations   4

Acknowledgements   5

Introduction   6

Suffolk enterprise: two centuries of change and adaptation   10

Index of companies   25

Lists of records   27

List of Illustrations

Gurteen's factory rules, c1877   7

William Pretty & Sons crèche, c1904   16

The machine shop at Robert Boby Ltd, 1924   37

Richard Garrett & Sons, Spanish advert   43

Smyth & Sons Peasenhall workshop, c1900   51

Cranfield's mill at Ipswich   58

Cranfield's delivery van, c1913   58

The annual garden party at R. & W. Paul, c1908   69

Paul's head office in 1912   73

Paul's cricket team, 1906   73

William Clowes first steam printing press   79

The composing room at Clowes   82

The biggest book in the world   83

Arnold & Gould's horsehair factory at Glemsford   86

Hand-loom weaving at the Gainsborough Silk Weaving Company   89

Female workers at Gurteen's factory, c1881   91

Almost a century later at Gurteens   92

Gurteen's hair weaving factory   93

Strand-laying at Haverhill Rope, Twine and Sack Company   94

William Pretty & Sons factory at Tower Ramparts, Ipswich   97

Corset stitching at William Pretty & Sons   99

Preparing rabbit skins at William Rought Ltd, Brandon, c1920   101

The Bark Yards at Webb & Sons' Combs Tannery, c1900   104

An advert for Gurteen's breeches, c1930   111

Acknowledgements

This survey has been made possible by a grant from the Ann Ashard Webb bequest to the School of History, University of East Anglia, for which we are most grateful. We have received help from many people during the preparation of this book: Bob Feltwell (Ipswich Chamber of Commerce), Jane Gooch (Museum of East Anglian Life, Stowmarket), Dee Crowe and Jenny Smith (Ipswich Women's History Group), Patrick Crouch (Haverhill and District Local History Society) and Bob Malster. All generously gave their time and expertise. The staff of the Suffolk Record Offices, especially Gwyn Thomas, Judith Tydeman, Jane Isaacs and Bill Wexler, have throughout given us much help and encouragement. Thanks are also due to Richard Wilson and Brian Seward who have read and commented on the text. Lastly, we are particularly grateful to the company executives and archivists who have welcomed us to their firms and given access to their records: Arnold & Gould; Sifbronze; Clays; William Clowes; Courtaulds (William Pretty & Sons); Cranfields; Gainsborough Silk Weaving Company; Glemsford Silk Mills; Gurteens; ICI (Stowmarket Paints Division); Muntons; Pauls Malt; Reckitt Benckiser (Suffolk Chemical Company); Unilever (Birds Eye Wall's) and Webb & Son (Combs).

Picture credits

The authors wish to thank the following for kind permission to reproduce illustrations:

Gurteens for Plates 1, 16-18, 24; Suffolk Record Office for Plates 2, 4 and 22; Museum of East Anglian Life, Stowmarket, for Plates 3, 5, 14, 19 and 23; Cranfields for Plates 6 and 7; Pauls Malt for Plates 8-10; Clowes for Plates 11-13; Gainsborough Silk Weaving Company for Plate 15; Ipswich Women's History Group for Plates 20 and 21.

Introduction

Business records are among the most under-utilised of archives, yet they represent some of the richest sources available to historians. The records of Suffolk companies, those deposited in the county's three record offices, in archives elsewhere, or held privately, are no exception. For those interested in researching the history of a company, in industrial archaeology, textile design and fashion, changing technology, or simply finding out about the working life of a family member, they offer a mine of information. More broadly, they provide an invaluable insight into the social and economic history of Suffolk during the last two hundred years.

The records themselves are widely varied and comprise ledgers and minute books, financial accounts, plans, photographs, tape recordings and artefacts. Of these, directors' minutes and, where it survives, correspondence, shed the greatest insight into the life of a firm: its ownership, organisation and administration. Financial records, given the many differences in accounting practice, can prove a minefield for historians. Nevertheless, besides an annual profit and loss account and balance sheet, they provide details of a company's capitalisation and valuations of its assets, including plant and stock. Many accounts give sales or turnover relating to individual departments or operations. As in the case of Pauls, this can give a unique insight into the relative importance and profitability of the company's interests, here malting, animal feedstuffs and shipping. Ledgers and journals come in a great variety, embracing personal, capital, sales and production and give a day-to-day record of the working life of the firm. Again, their use varied from company to company. Production records might include an actual log of production; accounts relating to raw materials (costs and stocks); wages; transport (including horses and stabling) and precisely calculated overall costings. The daybooks of some of the smaller companies contain a wealth of detail. Those of the Haverhill Rope, Twine and Sack company have precise drawings of every order for tarpaulins and lorry covers; those of the small west Suffolk engineering firm W.J. Ford & Sons record the family's 'alternative' occupation as local vets and their treatment of farm animals. Employment records, besides providing another measure of the size of the company, may include apprenticeship indentures, wage rates, hours of work and conditions; the factory rules of Gurteens (see Plate 1) were typical of those in force in numerous firms. Some companies provided pension schemes and a range of social and welfare benefits which, in the pre-welfare state era, proved invaluable. Oral evidence gives further insight into working lives, and the Suffolk Oral History Project has catalogued the large collection of tapes (including a section on occupations/crafts/industries) held by the

Suffolk Record Office. A second collection, focusing on women at work, is held by the Ipswich Women's History Group.

FACTORY
RULES AND REGULATIONS,
CHAUNTRY MILLS, HAVERHILL.

Abstract of Time, *(according to Factory Acts.)*

WORKING HOURS :--

Morning	.	from 6-15 to 8-15,	2 Hours		
Forenoon	.	,, 9 to 1	4 ,,	5 days	50 hours
Afternoon	.	,, 2 to 6	4 ,,		

SATURDAYS 6-15 to 8-15, 9 to 1, 6 ,,

56 Hours,

Time allowed for Cleaning ½-hour.

TOTAL . . . 56½ ,,

CLOSING of the Gates.

The GATES will be closed FIVE MINUTES after, viz:

6-20, Morning,

9-5, Forenoon,

2-5, Afternoon.

Entrance and Exit.

The Entrance and Exit to be TO and FROM the LODGE GATES and the Gates in the Croft, until the time for closing of the gates as above; after which the Entrance and Exit to be through the Lodge Gates only, until the next meal-time.

Admission after closing time.

The Lodge Gate will be re-opened at intervals, (as below,) to admit any who may have been Shut out; such person to lose half-an-hour, and to contribute one penny to the Sick fund:

Morning from 6-30 to 6-35. Forenoon 9-15 to 9-20. Afternoon 2.15 to 2-20.

After which time no admission will be granted until next Meal-time.

Any person found persisting in coming on or going from the premises in any other way or at any other time than specified by these Rules, to contribute SIXPENCE to the Sick fund, and liable to be discharged.

Loss of time.

All persons losing time without permission, to forfeit wages for such time, and also to contribute one penny per hour to the Sick fund.

Overtime,

OVERTIME without instructions will not be paid for. Overtime not to count until the 56½ hours are made in the week.

On and after the week ending JULY 19th, an account of all Work will be taken to Thursday Night, to be paid for the Saturday following.

July 12th, 1877.

J. BROMORE, Printer and Stationer, Haverhill.

Gurteen's factory rules, c1877

Besides these various classes of records generated by the businesses themselves, there are a number of other sources, which provide additional information relating to business and industrial history. Of these, trade directories and local newspapers, both dating back to the late eighteenth century, are easily accessible. The county Record Offices also hold good collections of modern newscuttings (indexed alphabetically at Ipswich and Lowestoft, by parish at Bury St Edmunds). District and urban council records include company plans for expansion, those of Sudbury, for instance, dating from the late nineteenth century. In the British Parliamentary Papers may be found statistical evidence and commissions of enquiry focused on specific industries. Brewing and malting, for example, were both subject to taxation, and a wealth of information helps to set the fortunes of these sectors in a wider context. The Boby Building (originally part of Robert Boby's Bury St Edmund's factory) at the Museum of East Anglian Life at Stowmarket houses displays of artefacts from a number of companies. Some firms have their own museums where they have similar displays; these are usually either open to the public or by private appointment.

The guide does not attempt to provide a comprehensive list of Suffolk companies and their records. Its content has been determined, primarily, by the survival of archives, and limited to manufacturing, although this has been interpreted broadly to include the processing of food and other agricultural products. (The exceptions are the ports of Felixstowe and Ipswich, a decision which reflects their major influence on the development of Suffolk business.) Business records are often at risk during mergers and take-overs and most seriously when firms are closed. Already the archives of many of the county's best-known firms have been lost or destroyed. Similarly, little is known about the majority of small firms. Here we have tried to provide a guide to the extant records and other relevant evidence (secondary literature, artefacts and oral records) of some of Suffolk's oldest established firms. Where major collections have already been listed in detail in other reference works, this has been indicated and a shortened list included. Several archives held privately by companies have been listed for the first time. The records are alphabetically arranged in five main sectors: chemical processing, engineering, food processing, printing, textiles and allied industries, plus a small miscellaneous section. The guide also includes an essay on the changing structure of business in Suffolk over the last two centuries. Finally, it must be remembered that further deposits of business records are continually received by the county's three Record Offices. Their excellent staff are always willing to help those interested in any aspect of business or related history.

Abbreviations used

SRO - Suffolk Record Office (I) Ipswich; (B) Bury St Edmunds (L) Lowestoft, numbers being the catalogue numbers in the respective offices.

NRA - *National Register of Archives,*
Guides vols 8 and 9 - volumes of *Records of British Business and Industry 1760-1914, volume 8, Textiles and Leather, and 9 Engineering and Metal work*, published by HMSO, numbers being the *item* number of the listed record in the respective volume.

Richmond and Stockford - L Richmond and B. Stockford, *Company Archives: the survey of the records of 1000 of the first registered companies.* (Gower, 1986), the number being the *item* number.

Richmond and Turton - L. Richmond and A. Turton (eds), *The Brewing Industry: a Guide to Historical Records* (Manchester University Press, 1990)

Other useful sources

J. Orbell, *A Guide to Tracing the History of a Business* (Gower, 1987)
The Past remembered: A Catalogue of Oral History Tapes, 3rd edition (Suffolk County Council, 1995)

Suffolk Enterprise:
Two Centuries of Change and Adaptation

In the medieval and early modern periods East Anglia was probably the richest region of England, the county of Suffolk prominent in the lucrative wool trade. Subsequently the economic and commercial history of the county has been associated with a rich agricultural sector but relative industrial stagnation as the 'Industrial Revolution' proceeded in the north and Midlands. In 1849 Suffolk was described as being 'wholly without manufactures'.[1] Certainly, by the early decades of the nineteenth century, little remained to indicate the extensiveness and wealth of the textile industry. As Yorkshire power looms superseded hand-loom weaving, the wool towns of south-west Suffolk were blighted by poverty and unemployment. Yet this bleak picture was by no means universal. Elsewhere, the county stood on the brink of unprecedented commercial expansion: in malting, milling and brewing, in printing, agricultural engineering, and the manufacture of fertilisers and ready-made clothes. Fifty years later, Suffolk boasted firms of national importance, their products renowned throughout the world. Agriculture remained the single most important sector. But the 're-industrialisation' of Suffolk during the second half of the nineteenth century marked a shift away from a narrow dependence on textiles to a diverse industrial base. It was a process of change and adaptation that was to continue after 1900; through depression, two World Wars, and the technological revolution that followed.

In large measure the decline of Suffolk's fortunes was a reflection of the 'Industrial Revolution': the region's lack of mineral reserves and remoteness from the focus of technical change. By the end of the eighteenth century, the county had neither the resources nor location to maintain its supremacy as a leading manufacturing centre. Subsequently, as contemporaries stressed, it was the predominant agricultural sector that was to form the foundations of the economy, providing employment and a base for industrial diversification. Agriculture was itself subject to significant pressures during the two centuries that followed, not least the periods of intense depression: following the Napoleonic Wars, from the mid-1870s and during the inter-war years. The result was prolonged and widespread rural poverty and the consequent exodus of labour (probably the most dynamic) to major industrial towns and the colonies and, from the 1850s, the steady depopulation of large areas of the countryside. More positively, low wages and land prices throughout much of the period, together with proximity to London, attracted new industries to the county. The other key factor influencing the business environment was communications. The county had gained from improved roads and navigations in the eighteenth century, but it was the development of the main ports and the coming of the railways from the mid-nineteenth century which, perhaps more than any other factor, did much to underpin recovery.

The ports had long been central to Suffolk's commerce, facilitating the coastal trade to London and the north-east and to more distant markets. By the end of the eighteenth century, however, conditions at some of the more important ones were poor. Despite the safety of their sheltered quays, their approaches were hazardous and prone to silting. Ipswich, once among the leading centres for wool exports, had long ago been described by Charles I as 'a haven without water'.[2] By the mid-eighteenth century sizeable ships, unable to reach the quays, were forced to load and discharge below the town. The corporation, like many another, complacent and corrupt, took little action. Not until 1805 were River Commissioners appointed to undertake improvements; it was 1837 before the Act authorising the wet dock was finally passed. Opened five years later and quickly complemented by the advent of the railway, the new dock transformed the fortunes of the town. For the first time the population of Ipswich exceeded that of Yarmouth as it steadily supplanted its old rival as the major East Anglian import and distribution centre.[3] Similar advances were repeated at Lowestoft. At the end of the eighteenth century it remained a small market and fishing town of some 2,000 inhabitants. The first harbour, part of a scheme to take sea-going vessels to Norwich, was completed in 1830. The project failed, but provided the basis for further expansion by the builder-entrepreneur, Samuel Morton Peto, and the opening in 1847 of the Lowestoft to Norwich Navigation. The coming of the railway and the construction of the Waveney Dock in 1883 provided the means to exploit the full potential of the fishing industry both for domestic and export markets. As at Ipswich, the town's population grew at an unprecedented rate, rising to over 13,000 in 1871 and almost trebling again in the next forty years. Suffolk's third major port, Felixstowe, developed more slowly, beginning in 1875 with the formation by George Tomline of the Felixstowe Dock and Railway Company. Initially overshadowed by Ipswich and Harwich, the dock reached its full potential in the twentieth century, ultimately becoming the leading UK container port.[4]

The modernisation of the ports coupled with good rail links to national markets formed the cornerstones of business revival. Not surprisingly many of the industries which subsequently flourished had their roots in agriculture and fishing. Some, like brewing and malting, were old established. In 1741, malt production in Suffolk exceeded that in any other excise collection district, and long before the nineteenth century local firms were prominent in the national market. By the 1840s Patrick Stead of Halesworth was considered the best maltster in England, a reputation based on the fine quality of local barley.[5] Milling, too, had a long tradition in the county. In 1830 William Cobbett found the windmills on the hills surrounding Ipswich 'so numerous that [he] counted whilst in one place no less than seventeen'.[6] In all, some 500 were at work in Suffolk, mainly grinding corn.[7] Small-scale malting and milling using local crops remained important throughout the county, but from the 1870s the cheap American and European grain flooding into the ports offered unprecedented opportunities. At Ipswich, the Paul brothers imported huge quantities of barley and maize, creating one of the largest British malting and animal feedstuffs companies. John and Thomas Cranfield erected their new roller mill beside the dock; the milling firm of E. Marriage & Son of Colchester were similarly attracted by facilities at Felixstowe. At Lowestoft the rapid expansion of the fishing industry (by 1913 there were 700 drifters and trawlers operating out of the port) sustained both old and new industries: rope and net-making, shipbuilding and marine engineering, while canning supplemented the export of cured and salted herrings, Maconachies and Mortons establishing the largest factories in Britain.[8]

The combination of local demand and access to distant markets again underpinned the development of Suffolk's heavy industries, the manufacture of chemical fertilisers and agricultural engineering. The former was begun by Edward Packard, a Saxmundham chemist, who initially produced superphosphates by dissolving finely ground bones in sulphuric acid. The discovery in 1843 of local supplies of coprolites, and the realisation of their importance as a raw material, subsequently underpinned the rapid growth of the trade. Soon after Packard moved his works from Snape to Bramford, near Ipswich, where in 1851 he built the first complete acid and superphosphate factory, thereby gaining the added advantages of good rail and sea communications. Together with Prentice Brothers of Stowmarket and Joseph Fison (who also moved to Bramford), he continued to dominate the keen local competition. And when supplies of coprolites were exhausted after 1880, these firms were ideally placed to import raw materials from the continent and for the export of a growing range of products - specialist horticultural and agricultural fertilisers, sheep dips, insecticides and disinfectants.[9]

More surprising, given the remoteness from its sources of coal and iron, was the rapid development of the engineering sector from the late eighteenth century. Initially, the trade met the demands of local agricultural markets. Robert Ransome, a Norfolk Quaker who moved to Ipswich in 1789 was the most famous of an outstanding group of entrepreneurs. His method of tempering cast iron plough shares, patented in 1785, the chilled plough share of 1803 and interchangeable plough parts which followed five years later were key innovations in the manufacture of ploughs. Subsequently the firm's products widened to include lawn mowers, railway equipment and structural ironwork. By 1850, Ransomes were said to be the largest manufacturers of metal goods in the country. The Orwell Works, built soon after the completion of the new dock, occupied eleven acres and employed well in excess of 1,000 men, around one in seven of the town's male workforce.[10] By this time, not only Ransomes, but Garretts of Leiston (founded in 1778), James Smyth of Peasenhall (1792), Whitmore & Binyon of Wickham Market (1780), Woods, Cocksedge & Warner of Stowmarket, and the Ipswich firm of E.R.& F.Turner, had established national and international reputations. Writing in 1872, Bayne reckoned 'their engines and implements may be found in every English county, in every country in Europe and in our colonies'.[11] The sector continued to grow: Robert Boby of Bury St Edmunds (founded in 1843) gained a fine reputation for their expertise as brewing and malting engineers, and Elliott and Garrood of Beccles (who also began as agricultural engineers) for their marine engines. The emphasis on exports, encouraged by the depression in agriculture from the mid-1870s, also increased. Many of these firms employed well versed specialist foreign travellers; sales literature was produced in a range of languages to suit the markets; technical specifications and designs were developed for particular market needs. Ransomes, for example, developed straw burning apparatus for steam engines for markets where coal was not readily available. By these means, Suffolk's engineers captured world-wide markets and by 1914 were exporting the greater part of their production.[12]

The success of engineering stood in marked contrast to the fortunes of the county's traditional staple industry, textiles. Attempts were made to introduce alternative occupations into south-west Suffolk, the worst affected region; strawplaiting for the hat trade flourished in the half century after 1830, at its peak in the 1870s employing well over 2,000 women and girls. A decade later, however, it had virtually disappeared.[13] The weaving of horsehair and coconut fibre proved more enduring; it was here that some strawplaiters subsequently found employment. The pool of cheap skilled labour also attracted new industries from outside the area. The earliest of these was silk processing, which migrated from London after the Spitalfields' Act of 1774 increased London weavers' wage rates. Suffolk was never as important as Norfolk as a silk producing area, but small centres did grow up at Sudbury, Haverhill and Glemsford, employing 2,000 hands at their peak in the mid-nineteenth century. A few specialist firms survived, but generally the industry enjoyed fluctuating fortunes and was unable to replace, at least in terms of employment, traditional textile manufacture. The greatest success in this respect came with diversification into ready-made clothing and was led by one of the county's oldest established firms, Gurteens of Haverhill. Founded c1784 by Daniel Gurteen, a merchant and weaver, by 1819 the company had begun to sell ready-to-wear smocks. The introduction of steam power in the 1850s enabled the shift to mechanised factory production and the manufacture of ready-made clothing for the working class market. By the late 1880s the firm was employing well over 3,000 workers and had become one of the largest clothing manufacturers in the country with extensive national and overseas markets.[14] Gurteens apart, however, the main focus of this growing industry was Ipswich. Initially based on out-working, the shift to factory production was achieved in the 1870s when W. Fraser & Company established a large workshop in St Margaret's Place. By the mid 1880s the business employed in excess of 1,000 and exported its products world-wide. Bugg & Company operated a similar business in Princes Street[15] while Phillips & Piper (who merged with another Ipswich Company, the London & East Anglian Tailoring Company, in 1900) specialised in high quality menswear and riding clothes, many of which were again exported. Corset making formed a further distinct branch of the industry and by the early 1900s the leading firm, William Pretty & Son, had opened branches throughout East Anglia and employed in all some 1,200 workers. Together these factories offered a major source of employment for women and girls, thus providing a valuable complement to the male-dominated engineering sector.

The concentration of the clothing industry in Ipswich again illustrates the general shift away from the countryside to the ports and main centres of urban growth. Several London companies were, however, attracted by cheap rural land and labour. In the 1870s William Clowes & Son acquired a small printing firm at Beccles as did Richard Clay at Bungay, both building up companies of national status. British Xylonite – the first company successfully to manufacture commercial plastic (celluloid) – similarly moved to Brantham in 1887. Elsewhere specialist industries survived. Brandon, with its Gun Flint Company and William Rought Limited, who prepared rabbit and hare skins for hat-making, boasted two of the more unusual. Garretts were the mainstay of Leiston, as were Gurteens at Haverhill. Indeed, the latter were said to employ almost everyone not engaged in agriculture.[16] Small scale industries and crafts were still to be found scattered throughout the county: tanning, brickmaking, sack and rope making, for example. But on the eve of the First World War Suffolk's industrial structure was characterised by large-scale modernised industries located in the major towns. Bury St Edmunds, the 'social' capital of the county, was home to the engineering company, Robert Boby, and to Greene King, a leading provincial brewer. Stowmarket supported a range of industries: explosives, malting, milling and brewing. But above all, it was the eastern ports, with their extensive import and export trade which had prospered: Lowestoft, by now

Suffolk's second town; but most notably, Ipswich, with its dominant engineering sector, manufacture of fertilisers, ready-made clothing and cigars, and its more traditional industries, brewing, malting and milling. It may not have conformed to preconceived notions of the 'Victorian industrial city', but it was, as Holderness concluded, 'upon any definition, industrial'.[17]

If location was a major factor in business revival, this responsiveness to changing market circumstances illustrates the adaptability of Suffolk's business and industrial leaders. The nineteenth century was an era when the family business dominated. Although several became limited companies in the late Victorian and Edwardian period the age of 'corporate capitalism' was to come only in the twentieth century. Risk taking and management of resources were the responsibility of individual entrepreneurs or their descendants. The level of enterprise displayed poses questions over what has become a stereotypical view of 'failure' in the business community in late Victorian Britain. The marketing methods of the agricultural engineers, as we have seen, contradict accusations of complacency in foreign markets. Indeed, many Suffolk businessmen looked overseas, often to America, for new ideas. William Paul and his son Stuart travelled extensively in the 1890s, establishing trading links and securing the latest technology, while John Cranfield, a farmer's son from Buckden in Huntingdon, gained milling experience in Minneapolis before setting up on his own account. There can be few better examples of an 'entrepreneurial family' than the Prentices of Stowmarket. Initially merchants and farmers, the family diversified into brewing and malting, then in the 1850s, began to manufacture chemical fertilisers (Prentice Brothers, later part of Fisons, was founded in 1856), took over the management of the town's gas supply, and set up the Patent Gun Cotton Company (later to become part of the ICI Paints Division). Of the next generation, Napier Prentice pioneered the production of quiet-running electric motors and generators; by the age of twenty-five he had built the generator to light the Paris Opera House, followed by those to supply lighting to Stowmarket, Diss and Felixstowe. He formed the East Anglian Engineering Company and in 1898 began the production of Bull Motors, a range which became an integral part of E.R.& F. Turner in 1932.[18]

The influence of the Protestant, particularly the non-conformist, ethic is also strongly evident. Many of the founding businessmen were Quakers or followers of other non-conformist confessions.[19] The first census of Church attendance in 1851 showed that most of the adult population attended regular services, but that non-conformism was strongest in the chief manufacturing districts.[20] By implication these were more likely to be the industrial towns of the north and Midlands. But a long history of religious dissent meant that the work ethic and notion of 'improvement' commonly associated with

Samuel Smiles,[21] were equally evident in Suffolk. The chapel and meeting house enforced a strict moral code of business practice and offered practical and financial help. George Paul, for example, secured a business loan of £20 after he moved to Bury St Edmunds in the 1770s.[22] Like the Pauls, a striking number of Suffolk businessmen were members of the Independent (later Congregational) Church: the Prentices and Hewitts of Stowmarket, the Crisps of Beccles, the Ipswich families of Byles, Fison, Pretty and Armstrong (who succeeded to the Cranfield business) and, at Haverhill, the Gurteens.[23] Their families worshipped together, participated in the many activities of the church, intermarried and established close business links. The Quakers were also well represented, and it is clear that the far-reaching hand of their extensive network stretched well beyond local boundaries. In 1840 Ransome money was instrumental in assisting Isaac Reckitt of Hull in the formation of the business that was to become the world's largest supplier of household starch and polish.[24] Thirty years later the Ransomes provided finance to enable two young Americans, Edward Bradley and J. Sheldon, to establish the first mechanised brushmaking company in Britain.[25] Many of these businessmen were equally concerned with the moral improvement and welfare of their workers. In the 1850s Ransome's Mental Improvement Society's evening classes attracted between 200-300 of their workforce.[26] William Pretty, who provided a canteen and crèche for his women workers was renowned as a paternalistic employer, while at Haverhill, Daniel Gurteen established a mat-making factory in 1886 specifically to provide employment at a time of deep agricultural depression.[27] Widely involved in civic life and major benefactors to their towns, the work of these entrepreneurs demonstrates the importance of their success to the well being and prosperity of the communities in which they lived.

William Pretty & Sons were renowned as paternalistic employers and provided a range of benefits, including this crèche (c1904), for their female workers.

For most industries and firms, the First World War marked a watershed. To some degree, all had to cope with shortages of labour and raw materials, government controls and the disruption of markets. Many turned to war-work: Ransomes, despite their Quaker origins, made aeroplanes, the Stowmarket explosives company, guncotton and cellulose syrup for aircraft 'dopes', its workforce rising to over 3,000. But if war was profitable, any optimism for the future was short-lived as depression quickly set the pattern for the inter-war years. Some of the hardest hit were the engineering firms. Their major markets in Russia, continental Europe and Latin America had been largely lost while the depression in arable farming brought a further fall in domestic demand. Garretts were one of eleven companies forced into (unsuccessful) amalgamation, and from 1919 Robert Boby effectively became a subsidiary of Vickers. During these years rationalisation and merger was widespread throughout British industry. In Suffolk few sectors bucked the trend. Edward Packard & Company acquired the Thetford fertiliser business of James Fison in 1919 and ten years later merged with Prentice Brothers to form Fison, Packard and Prentice. Control of the Lowestoft coachbuilding firm, United Automobile Services, passed to Tilling & British Automobile Traction Ltd and LNER, the company subsequently merging with three other regional firms to form Eastern Counties Omnibus Company. William Pretty & Son was taken over by the Market Harborough firm of R.&W.H. Symmington; Adnams and Greene King acquired smaller breweries while the number of Suffolk malting companies affiliated to the Maltsters' Association fell in the two decades after 1919 from 28 to 12.[28] These figures reflect not only the wave of mergers, but the other main feature of the period - the collapse of those small companies who, unable to withstand depressed conditions, ceased trading. Yet new companies were successfully established: the Suffolk Iron Foundry (now Atco-Qualcast), started in 1920 by Louis John Tibbenham; Muntona (now Muntons), specialising in malt extract and malt products; and in 1926 the engineering firm, Cranes, which delayed opening for six years because of the recession and then struggled to meet demand.[29] And despite the crisis in farming, agriculture continued to provide a basis for industrial diversification. The widespread cultivation of sugar beet, the salvation of many an East Anglian farmer, prompted the building of processing factories at Ipswich and Bury St Edmunds. Vegetable canning was introduced at Woodbridge, bacon curing at Elmswell, while the development of compound feeds (encouraged by the increase in poultry rearing) was the main focus of growth for Pauls. The production of artificial silk was started at Lowestoft and Stowmarket (where the project failed) while for Prettys the manufacture of artificial silk underwear put them once again at the forefront of world markets.

The picture was not one of unrelieved gloom, but fortunes varied widely across the county. What was evident was a continuation of trends observed before 1914: a greater centralisation of industry into larger scale units. Small rural firms, as in malting, did particularly badly. Improvements in road transport and electrification were beneficial. But unemployment and low incomes in agriculture blighted local markets and encouraged the exodus from rural areas, a vicious circle that diminished their attractiveness. Proximity to larger industrial centres offering a better range and quality of professional services, specialised ancilliary industries and technical education,[30] was increasingly important. A survey of industry in the country towns of Norfolk and Suffolk found that virtually all the growth (in terms of employment) during the 1930s was achieved by firms controlled by or linked to external companies, those with access to greater capital, technical and managerial resources.[31] Such factors helped to underpin the expansion of industry (and population) at Stowmarket and Woodbridge which both benefited from the accessibility of Ipswich. The new port (and resort) of Felixstowe saw its population almost triple in the two decades after 1911.[32] In contrast, most other small towns, Eye, Framlingham, Halesworth, Saxmundham and Hadleigh among them, continued to decline.

As in the Great War the second international conflict brought innovations and adaptations to meet extraordinary need. Weapons of war, including aeroplanes and tanks, were manufactured in plants more accustomed to making lawn mowers or railway equipment: ploughshares were turned into swords. Physical destruction was also a constant threat. Cranes, a major munitions supplier, became a prime target for German bombers while the entire Eastern Coach Works was evacuated from Lowestoft, one of the most heavily bombed towns in the country, to the relative safety of Irthlingborough in Northamptonshire. More positively, these years restored many firms to profitability and turned thoughts to post-war reconstruction. Initially this was hindered by the continuation of rationing and government controls. But generally, once austerity eased, the 1950s and 60s were years of growth and relative prosperity, marked in many towns by the introduction of new firms and industries. At Lowestoft, the small packing unit leased in 1949 by Birds Eye Foods became a large frozen food factory, processing fish, fruit and vegetables. The Swiss shoe firm, Bally, who also came to the town shortly after the war, opened a new factory in 1955, while in 1951 Pye TV moved into a disused artificial silk factory, initially producing radios for export. By 1957 the workforce numbered 1,250.[33] With the discovery of North Sea gas and oil in the 1960s the town also developed into an important off shore supply and support centre, attracting such companies as Shell UK Exploration and SLP Engineering, specialists in sub-sea systems and the construction of offshore modules.[34] In West Suffolk the growing influence of planning policy played a significant role in reversing the region's decline.

The County Council, faced with an ageing population and shrinking economy, seized upon the opportunities offered by the 1952 Town Development Act. Agreements were reached with the Greater London Council for development schemes at Haverhill and Bury St Edmunds and, on a smaller scale, at Sudbury, Mildenhall, Brandon and Newmarket.[35] The GLC built large housing estates to relocate London families, with the Urban District Council investing in factory units. Public investment stimulated private, and by the mid-1960s around 120 new factories, catering for a broad range of industries, had been built, and about 1,600 new jobs in manufacturing were being created each year.[36]

Some established firms, especially those catering for a bygone age, found the post-war climate less favourable. John George & Sons of Whelnetham, who made hand tools, the Peasenhall engineers, James Smyth & Sons, and William Rought, the hatter's furriers, all closed during the 1960s, the victims of changing technology or fashion. Notably, all three faced the additional problem of rural location. Many small concerns similarly found the costs of modernisation beyond their reach. Malting, for example, became a high technology sector by the 1970s and the smaller firms were forced to choose between leaving the industry or approaching a larger competitor. The Ipswich Malting Company joined Associated British Maltsters; in 1958, S. Swonnell & Sons of Oulton Broad were acquired by Pauls who had initiated a major expansion programme following their public flotation in 1960. In the same way Cranfields purchased local millers and invested in bakeries, becoming the largest privately owned milling-bakery group in the country. In 1972, however, they were themselves taken over by Associated British Foods. Other sectors, brewing, printing, textiles, engineering and food processing, were similarly affected as long established, often family firms, relinquished their independence. As in the inter-war years, merger was a national phenomenon, marking a period of significant concentration throughout British industry.[37]

Undoubtedly, one of the most important developments of the period was the growth of the port of Felixstowe. During the war the port was occupied by the Royal Navy and Air Force and by the end of hostilities was run down to the extent that its future remained uncertain. However, in 1951 the company was purchased by H. Gordon Parker for £50,000, largely because it remained outside the National Dock Labour Scheme and achieved comparatively high levels of productivity. Pioneering work on the bulk storage of liquids was followed by the development of cargo handling techniques that were to revolutionise the shipping and ports industry. Roll-on, roll-off services were developed from the mid-1960s and the first container terminal was completed in 1968. Seven years later the company joined European Ferries and by the early 1980s had become the leading UK container port. This success nevertheless highlighted the region's need for much improved road links, particularly to the Midlands. Indeed, the only route for much of the traffic destined for Felixstowe was through the centre of Ipswich, Stowmarket and Bury St Edmunds, causing severe congestion and increasing problems for the business community. Plans for a by-pass and bridge over the river Orwell were first proposed in 1965. The following year, as part of government strategy for the south-east, Ipswich became the subject of development plans which included these improvements. But three years later, with policy shifting towards the building of new towns, the scheme was dropped.[38] Thereafter the task of resolving the problem rested with local initiative, in particular the Chamber of Trade and the newly formed Ipswich Industrial Group. After a lengthy campaign and public inquiry, the Orwell river bridge and southern by-pass were finally opened in December 1982. The western by-pass to the A14 followed after a second public inquiry, linking the Midlands with Felixstowe and Europe, and providing an immense stimulus not only to the port of Felixstowe, but also to Ipswich and its immediate hinterland.[39]

From the mid-1970s, however, industry throughout Britain was feeling the effects of a much harsher economic climate. Escalating fuel costs following the 1973 oil crisis and a surge in cheap foreign imports had hit most sectors. The sharp recession of the early Thatcher years and the booms and slumps which followed decimated large swathes of manufacturing industry across the country. Generally Suffolk fared better than many other regions, but the two main urban areas, Ipswich and the north east, both heavily dependent upon traditional manufacturing industry, suffered badly.[40] Lowestoft, disadvantaged by its remoteness and poor communications, and with an economy dominated by a small number of large firms (almost all owned by large corporations), inevitably proved susceptible. The closure of Pye TV by Phillips Electronics in 1980 was partly cushioned by the reopening of the factory the following year by Sanyo. But one after another, the town lost most of its major firms: Eastern Coach Works, as part of the rationalisation of British Leyland, in 1987; Mortons, after its acquisition by Hillsdown Holdings, the following year; Bally's Shoe Factory in 1990;[41] the two shipbuilding companies, Richards and Brooke Yachts (formerly Brooke Marine), both founded in 1873, in 1993 and 1994 respectively; and the Co-operative Canning Factory (acquired by Chivers Hartley in 1994) three years later.[42] During the same period, the fishing industry, the victim of increasing European legislation, similarly contracted. Unemployment in the town, which in 1971 had stood at 3.5 per cent, peaked at 17 per cent in 1987, fell sharply, only to rise again from the beginning of the 1990s and to remain above the regional average.[43] High unemployment was matched by low wages, which in turn deterred the growth of the service sector thus hindering structural change. The smaller towns in the district, equally disadvantaged, experienced a similar fate. Such was the scale of the problem that the Waveney district (including Lowestoft, Bungay, and Halesworth), together with two other isolated rural towns, Eye and Stradbroke, attracted increasing government and European Commission funding aimed at economic and social regeneration and culminating, in 1999, in Assisted Area status.[44]

To a lesser extent, the same pressures were felt at Ipswich. Many old-established firms were closed: the textile companies, Phillips & Piper and William Pretty; A.J. Turner, the tanning firm established in 1716; Ransomes & Rapier; Burton Son & Sandars and Churchmans, the cigar manufacturers. The closure of Cranfields in the last month of the century left the wet dock, for so long the centre of the town's prosperity, almost devoid of industry, a symbolic event that perhaps more than any other underlines the extent of structural change during these years.[45] But Ipswich, with its larger, diverse economy, proved more resilient and better able to adapt. A major factor was its good communications. The rail and road network, together with the two ports: Ipswich, itself a leading short-sea container port specialising in the bulk handling of agricultural products, and Felixstowe, by now one of Europe's largest container ports, provided excellent access to national and international markets. Indeed, it was for this reason that new engineering firms like Celestion and Boulter were attracted to the town.[46] High technology companies, Hewlett Packard (who export 90 per cent of their output) and BT, whose research laboratories employ in excess of 3,000, also helped to offset the loss of declining sectors. Services, including finance and insurance, and those linked to the Port of Felixstowe, played an increasing role in the town's economy. The growth of business and retail parks, and the establishment of call centres (AXA group and Anglia Countrywide), all indicate a radical transformation in business culture.[47]

In varying degrees, these events were repeated across the county. Location and communications, as the contrasting fortunes of the north-east and the Ipswich region demonstrate, remained important determinants of prosperity, tempered, to some extent, by the increasing role of government and European aid. But everywhere the reliance on manufacturing and agriculture continued to decline, with the service sector enjoying the fastest growth. In 1997, services accounted for over 70 per cent of employment in the county, against 20 per cent in manufacturing and a mere 3 per cent in agriculture and fishing.[48] These figures broadly reflect national trends and the on-going process of structural change. Within that process, firms are born and die; growth sectors become declining ones; and technology is replaced by further advances. In Suffolk, as elsewhere, this involved the loss of many well-known firms. Yet one of the best indications of the underlying strength of Suffolk industry has been the survival of some of the county's oldest companies, not least those working in traditional manufacturing. The engineering sector, including Textron (formerly Ransomes), established in 1789, and E.R. & F. Turner, founded in 1837, continues to thrive, its products ranging from lawn mowers and flaking mills to fibre optic components. In printing, food processing, malting and brewing, Suffolk companies like Clays, Pauls Malt and Greene King, have remained at the forefront of their respective industries. And in west Suffolk, a cluster of companies, specialising in silk weaving and processing and the production of ready-made clothes, have maintained the county's long tradition in textiles. Unlike Gurteens (founded c1784) a family firm through seven generations, few have maintained their independence. But a growing number have secured their future through management buy-outs: the Tollemache & Cobbold Brewery, the printers, Clowes, Vanners and BOCM Pauls.[49] For nearly two hundred years, longer in some cases, these firms have demonstrated their resilience: throughout wars and depression and the technological revolution of recent decades. At the start of the twenty-first century, they remain at the heart of Suffolk's economy. They have been joined by newer concerns; the high technology companies (such as Hewlett Packard and Sanyo); and the many small firms beginning their lives on the business parks which have replaced out-dated town centre sites. Throughout the period, the county's ports, Lowestoft (which despite its difficulties remains a premier fishing port and centre for off-shore supplies), Ipswich, and the great post-war success, Felixstowe, have continued to play their key role in providing the gateways to world markets. Together they have been instrumental in placing Suffolk once again at the centre of one of the fastest growing regions in Britain.

1   William and Hugh Rainbird, *Agriculture in Suffolk* (1849), quoted in A. Betterton and D. Dymond, *Lavenham: industrial town* (1989), p. 75.

2   W.G. Arnott, *Orwell Estuary: The Story of Ipswich River*, (1954) p. 60.

3   The populations of Ipswich and Great Yarmouth in 1841 were 25,384 and 24,086 respectively and in 1851, 32,914 and 30,879; P. Corfield, 'The Social and Economic History of Norwich 1650-1850: A Study of Urban Growth', (PhD, University of London, 1976), pp. 396-97.

4   The history of the port of Felixstowe is well told by Robert Malster, *Felixstowe, 1886-1986: 100 Years a Working Port* (1986).

5   C.C. Owen, *The Greatest Brewery in the World: A History of Bass, Ratcliff & Gretton* (1992), p.50; See also R.Lawrence, 'An Early Nineteenth-Century Malting Business in East Suffolk', *Proceedings of the Suffolk Institute of Archaeology*, 36 (1986).

6   Quoted in B.A. Holderness, 'Pauls of Ipswich' (typescript, c1980), chapter two, p.3.

7   Peter Dolman, 'Windmills and Watermills', in David Dymond and Edward Martin (eds), *An Historical Atlas of Suffolk* (1999), p.148.

8   Peter Clements, *Lowestoft Through the Twentieth Century* (Lowestoft, 1999), p. 17; A.R. Charlesworth, *The Morton Story: The Lowestoft Food Factory 1901-1988* (privately published, 1995).

9   William Page (ed), *The Victoria History of the Counties of England: A History of Suffolk*, vol II, pp.285-6.

10 Peter Bishop, *The History of Ipswich: 1500 Years of Triumph and Disaster* (London, 1995), p.122.

11 A.D. Bayne, *Royal Illustrated History of Eastern England* (c1872), p.300.

12 See Roger Munting, 'Ransomes in Russia: an English Agricultural Engineering Company's Trade

with Russia to 1917', *Economic History Review*, Second series, XXXI, 1978, pp.257-269, for the best coverage of this trade.

13 Dymphna Crowe, 'Women in Industry: Aspects of female Employment in Suffolk and North Essex', *Suffolk Review*, 29, 1997, p. 17

14 Sara Payne, The Gurteens of Haverhill: Two Hundred Years of Suffolk Textiles (Cambridge, 1984), p.38.

15 William Page (ed), *Victoria History*, vol II, p. 276.

16 Gillian Holman, 'The Survival of a Suffolk Manufacturer, Gurteens, 1850 to 1900' (MA Dissertation, Winchester School of Art, 1995), p. 12.

17 B.A. Holderness, 'Pauls of Ipswich', chapter two, p. 1

18 The East Anglian Engineering Company became a member of 'Agricultural and General Engineers', a parent company controlling the interests of several East Anglian firms. When this venture failed in 1931, Bull Motors became part of E.R.& F.Turner Ltd. *The History of Engineering in Ipswich* (1949 edition), pp.72-75; Press cuttings and typescript notes on the history of the ICI Paint Division, HC 411/5/5 and 6; John Glyde, 'Materials for a History of Stowmarket', Misc and cuttings, Stowmarket 9, SRO (Ipswich).

19 This lends supports to the theories of Tawney and M. Weber. Weber's, *The Protestant Ethic and the Spirit of Capitalism*, was first published in article form in Germany in *Archiv für Sozialwissenschaft und Sozialpolitik*, xx (1904) and xxi (1905). The English translation, by Talcot Parsons, was published in 1926. Weber's ideas were influenced by the context in fast industrialising, Protestant Germany, but have a universal ring and might readily be applied to nineteenth century Britain. The argument was developed by R.H. Tawney in *Religion and the Rise of Capitalism* (1926).

20 Reported in J.F.C. Harrison, *Early Victorian Britain, 1832-1851* (1971), p.124. Sixty per cent of the population who could practically do so attended a place of worship. For most this meant the Anglican Church. The findings would tend to confirm a crude relation between non-conformity and industrial growth.

21 His *Self Help* was published in 1869 and sold a quarter of a million copies in his lifetime.

22 Whiting Street Chapel, Subscriptions and Accounts, FK 3/502/28, SRO (Bury).

23 Many of these families worshipped together at Tackett Street Church, Ipswich. The church records and census returns illustrate how close their relationships were. Marriages between the families were common, involving the Prentices, Fisons, Crisps, Hewitts, Pauls and Prettys; FK 3/502/52-3, 3/502/28, SRO (Ipswich), *Census Returns* of Ipswich and Stowmarket.

24 Isaac Reckitt married Ann Coleby, daughter of Charles Coleby, a Norfolk corn merchant, in 1818. The family were devout Quakers. Her sister Sarah married Robert Ransome; two other sisters married businessmen, the three brothers-in-law all providing loans to Isaac; D. Chapman-Houston, *Sir James Reckitt: A Memoir* (1927), pp. 52-3, 65, 69.

25 The business was founded in 1869. It was registered in 1874 as the Star Brush Company, with Robert Ransome as its first chairman. Shares were also held by James Ransome and, later, Elizabeth Ransome. Capital was provided by two other agricultural engineers, Daniel Pidgeon of Banbury, and Alfred Crosskill of Beverley; Register of Members, Star Brush Company, Harrow Museum and Heritage Centre; 'The Rise of the Star Brush Company', *Brushes and Toilet Goods*, 1936, p. 12.

26 The Society was proposed by Allen Ransome in 1848 to provide 'Mental improvement, social intercourse and innocent recreation'. Established as the Ipswich Young Men's Association, it provided evening classes in mathematics, reading and writing, history, drawing and bookkeeping. The History of Engineering in Ipswich, p. 26; Peter Bishop, *The History of Ipswich: 1500 Years of Triumph and Disaster*, p. 122.

27 Gillian Holman, 'Gurteens', pp. 38-9.

28 Membership Lists, Maltsters' Association of Great Britain, Newark-upon-Trent.

29 *The History of Engineering in Ipswich*, pp. 113-14.

30 Ipswich had a long tradition of engineering education beginning with the Mechanics Institute founded in 1824. A Working Men's College was established in 1861, followed by the Municipal Technical School after the 1902 Education Act. In the inter-war years a School of Engineering was added to meet the growing demand for skilled engineering staff, the local engineering firms providing both funding and equipment. *The History of Engineering in Ipswich*, pp. 26-27.

31 T. Eastwood, *Industry in the Country Towns of Norfolk and Suffolk* (OUP, 1951), pp. 22-23.

32 The population of Felixstowe increased from 4,440 in 1911 to 12,067 by 1931. *Census Returns*, 1911, 1931.

33 Peter Clements, *Lowestoft Through the Twentieth Century*, pp. 47-48.

34 SLP Engineering (Sea and Land Pipelines) was established at Great Yarmouth in 1967. It set up at Lowestoft in 1971, with a base on the Ellough Industrial Estate. In 1980 the company acquired the Hamilton Yard at Lowestoft Harbour for the construction of offshore modules. *Docks*, 3, 1980.

35 The plan for Haverhill, signed in 1957, envisaged the doubling of the town's population to 9,750 but this was later doubled again to 18,500. By the mid 1960s besides the housing programme, new schools, shops, health and other social facilities had been built. The town had a new relief road and 37 new factories. Derek Senior, *Industry Thrives in West Suffolk* (1966), p. 18.

36 David Dymond and Peter Northeast, *A History of Suffolk* (1985), p. 116.

37 Between 1948 and 1973, 9,761 manufacturing firms disappeared through merger, no fewer than 8,066 in the period 1959-73. L. Hannah, *The Rise of the Corporate Economy* (1976), pp. 176-77.

38 Peter Bishop, *History of Ipswich*, p. 188.

39 Pauls *Link*, March 1983, p. 4.

40 By the early 1980s the north-east was the most industrialised district in Suffolk with a higher proportion of its workforce in manufacturing than in Britain as a whole. Waveney District Council, *The Waveney Local Plan* (1996), p. 69; E.E. Barritt, *Tomorrow's Suffolk* (1983).

41 The company was hit by the shift to synthetic shoes and cheap imports from third world countries. A small 'closing' unit was maintained at Lowestoft. *East Anglian Daily Times*, 12.9.1990.

42 After 1994 the factory operated under the Barber Richmore name.

43 Waveney District Council, *The Waveney Local Plan* (1996)

44 North-east Suffolk was designated a Rural Development Area in 1985. Halesworth and Bungay were awarded European Objective 5b funding in 1994. Together with Eye and Stradbroke, they also received funding from the government's Single Regeneration Budget in 1999. The Waveney Local Plan (1996), p.69; *Eastern Daily Press*, 16 July 1999.

45 Only Paul's Albion Malting remains operational. Plans for the regeneration of the wet dock include residential and leisure facilities. Paul's Stoke Maltings in Felaw Street (closed in 1980) have already been developed as a multi-purpose business centre and are now home to the Suffolk Chamber of Commerce.

46 Celestion, specialists in loudspeakers, was established at Hampton Wick in 1924 but relocated to Ipswich in 1968 to gain extra space and to be close to the ports. Boulter, the UK's leading manufacturer of oil-fired boilers, moved to Ipswich from Norwich in the late 1980s to take advantage of the better national and international communications. *Engineering Manufacturing in Ipswich* (Ipswich Borough Council), pp.2, 4.

47 *Engineering Manufacturing in Ipswich*, p.9; *Ipswich: opportunities for your business* (Ipswich Borough Council, 1999).

48 *Suffolk Business Directory, 2000* (Suffolk County Council), pp.34, 41-47.

49 Pauls was acquired by Harrisons & Crosfield in 1985. Pauls Malt was sold to the Irish conglomerate Greencore, in April 1998. Pauls Agriculture acquired BOCM in 1992 to become BOCM Pauls Ltd, then was the subject of a management buy-out in 1999. George Paul, the fifth generation of the family, again became chairman of the new company, Agricola Holdings.

Index of Companies

Adnams & Company plc, Southwold, Brewing	52
Arnold & Gould, Glemsford, Horsehair manufacture	86
Atco-Qualcast Ltd, Stowmarket, Lawn mower manufacture	36
Edward Baker Ltd, Great Cornard, Flour milling and pet foods	53
Birds Eye Wall's Ltd, Lowestoft, Frozen foods	54
Robert Boby, Bury St Edmunds, Agricultural and malting engineering	37
Brandon Gun Flint Company, Brandon, Gun flint manufacture	106
British Sugar, Bury St Edmunds, Sugar processing	55
British Sugar, Ipswich, Sugar processing	55
British Xylonite, Brantham, Chemicals and plastics	27
Burton, Son & Sandars, Ipswich, Confectionary supplies	56
John Chambers Ltd, Lowestoft, Shipbuilding and marine engineering	38
Churchmans Ltd, Ipswich, Cigarette and cigar manufacture	106
Clays Ltd, Bungay, Printing	79
William Clowes Ltd, Beccles, Printing	81
Cocksedge & Company Ltd, Ipswich, Structural and general engineering	39
Cooperative Wholesale Society Canning Factory, Lowestoft, Food preserving	57
W.S. Cowell Ltd, Ipswich, Printing	84
Cranfield Brothers Ltd, Ipswich, Milling and baking	57
John Crisp & Son Ltd, Beccles, Malting	60
G.& J. Cutting, Pettaugh, Milling	61
Eastern Coach Works Ltd, Lowestoft, Bus and coach bodybuilding	40
Elliott & Garrood Ltd, Beccles, Marine engineering	41
Felixstowe Dock & Railway Company, Transport and communications	107
Firmin & Company, Ipswich, Sacking manufacture	87
W.J. Ford & Sons, West Row, Mildenhall, Agricultural engineering	43
Gainsborough Silk Weaving Company Ltd, Sudbury, Silk weaving	88
Richard Garrett Engineering Ltd, Leiston, Agricultural engineering	43
John George & Sons Ltd, Welnetham, Bury St Edmunds, Hand tool manufacture	109
Glemsford Silk Mills, Glemsford, Silk throwsters and dyers	90
Green & Company, Lowestoft, Printing	85
Greene King & Sons, Bury St Edmunds, Brewing	61

D. Gurteen & Sons Ltd, Haverhill, Clothing manufacture — 91

Haverhill Rope, Twine & Sack Company, Haverhill, Rope and tarpaulin manufacture — 94

ICI Paints Division, Stowmarket, Paint manufacture — 29

Ind Coope Ltd, Halesworth, Brewing — 63

Ipswich Malting Company Ltd, Ipswich, Malting — 63

Ipswich Port Authority, Transport and communications — 110

Kirby-Warrick Pharmaceuticals Ltd, Mildenhall, Pharmaceuticals — 31

Lavenham Sugar Company, Sugar processing — 64

B.F. Marriage, Pakenham, Milling — 64

Charles Marston & Sons, Bungay, Milling — 65

J.C. Mauldon & Sons, Sudbury, Brewing — 65

E.& G. Morse, Lowestoft, Brewing — 66

C. & E. Morton Ltd, Lowestoft, Canning and preserving — 66

Muntons plc, Stowmarket, Malting and malt products — 67

Norsk Hydro Fertilisers Group (formerly Fisons plc) , Ipswich, Fertilisers — 32

Pauls Malt Ltd, Kentford, Malting — 69

J.E. Pettit & Sons, Redgrave, Milling — 74

Phillips & Piper Ltd, Ipswich, Clothing manufacture — 95

William Pretty & Sons, Ipswich, Corset and lingerie manufacture — 97

Ransomes plc (now Textron), Ipswich, Agricultural engineering — 45

Ransomes & Rapier plc, Ipswich, Industrial engineering — 48

William Rought Ltd, Brandon, Hatters' furriers — 99

Harry Rumsby & Sons, Bungay, Iron and brass founders — 111

James Smyth & Sons Ltd, Peasenhall, Agricultural engineering — 49

C.K. Squirrell & Sons Ltd, Bildeston, Malting and corn products — 74

Patrick Stead, Halesworth, Malting — 74

S. Swonnell & Son Ltd, Oulton Broad, Malting — 75

Suffolk Chemical Company Ltd, Ipswich, Industrial chemicals — 35

Tollemache & Cobbold Brewery Ltd, Ipswich, Brewing — 76

W. & A.J. Turner Ltd, Ipswich, Tanning — 100

H. Underwood & Sons Ltd, Ipswich, Leather and footwear manufacture — 101

Vanners, Sudbury, Silk weaving — 102

Watney Mann & Truman Maltings Ltd, Bungay, Malting — 78

Webb & Son (Combs) Ltd, Stowmarket, Tanning — 103

W.E. Wigg & Son, Barnby, Agricultural engineering — 51

CHEMICAL PROCESSING

British Xylonite Company Ltd, Brantham
Chemicals and plastics

The company was incorporated in 1877 at Homerton, Hackney - the first to make commercial plastic (celluloid). This had been invented, and patented in 1856, by Alexander Parkes and displayed in 1862 as 'Parkesine'. The product was clear and therefore could take any dye or pattern of finish (such as tortoiseshell). It had the great drawback, however, of being highly inflammable. The first firm to market the product was founded in 1865 by Parkes and Daniel Spill as the 'Parkesine Company Ltd'. It went into liquidation in 1868; Spill set up Xylonite in 1869 to manufacture 'Xylonoidine' on the old premises. This too was liquidated in 1874 and Spill opened Daniel Spill and Company in Homerton. He was joined by Levi Parsons Merriam in 1876; in 1877 the company was incorporated as the Xylonite Company Ltd. In 1887 the firm moved to Brantham because of the need to find more space. The site was chosen because it had both river and rail transport links, but particularly because of its cost, £4,000. A factory was built on Brookland Farms together with housing for about 150 workers who moved from London. The Xylonite raw material produced there continued to be made into finished goods in Hackney until 1897 when the works moved to a new factory in Hale End near Walthamstow, using the trade name of 'Halex'. Following the First World War the firm undertook research to find a non-flammable alternative to Xylonite. It also developed cellulose-acetate for photographic film. Subsidiary companies were opened in Canada 1922, and Australia 1931. Also in 1931 the company took over Cascelloid Ltd which made toys at Coalville in Leicestershire. The Brantham factory produced raw materials, mainly Xylonite but also Bexoid (cellulose acetate).

The Ipswich records show that in 1938 British Xylonite became a holding company with three subsidiaries: British Xylonite Plastics, Halex Ltd and Cascelloid Ltd (which made toys and bottles at Leicester and Coalville). There appears to be a minor inconsistency on this point. Richmond and Stockford suggest that in 1939 two subsidiary companies were formed: BX Plastics, which took over the raw material plants, and Halex Ltd which took over manufacture at Hale End. In 1939 the Distillers Company bought a fifty per cent share and the remainder in 1961. BX Plastics expanded its interests through acquisition during and after World War II, to include film and plastic jewellery and sheeting businesses. (A separate company, Bexford Ltd, was formed in 1946 together with Ilford Ltd to produce photographic film.) In 1951 BX Plastics bought back the manufacturing interests from Halex Ltd and others, which became marketing companies. In 1963 a new grouping called Bakelite Xylonite Ltd (jointly owned by Distillers and Union Carbide of New York) was formed from Bakelite Ltd, British Xylonite, BX Plastics and other UK companies owned by Union Carbide. In 1973 it sold the Brantham site to British Industrial Plastics (a subsidiary of Turner and Newell). In 1977 this was bought by Storey Brothers of Lancaster. The Brantham site operates as Wardle Storeys - until recently it made limited quantities of Xylonite using traditional processes. [In 1978 Bakelite Xylonite became a wholly owned subsidiary of British Petroleum Ltd.]

Records deposited at SRO (I) HC 410:

This is one of the most extensive holdings in SRO (I) (deposited 1981 and 1988). The catalogue alone is 139 pp. and is excellently clearly set out. It also has an extensive index of principal persons and organisations. The following is therefore a brief summary.

The records include British Xylonite Company Ltd from 1877 and British Xylonite Plastics from 1939 from the Brantham site: site, buildings and plant records: evidence of title, registers of capital expenditure, fire insurance records, building, development and railways sidings records, Brantham New Village; administration and letter books, 1869-1967: BX Company, general letter books, and other correspondence; Directors working papers: minutes, 1932-42; annual reports and accounts, 1888-1933, 1945-62; factory reports, general ledger 1965-9; production records; machinery notes and building registers, Brantham, 1908-37; output salaries and cost book, 1869-87, 1928-34; technical and laboratory records 1882-1937, 1924-42: papers of professor John Attfield, formula books and laboratory reports press cuttings, records re inflammability of celluloid, records on German plastics industry in Second World War; competitor review, analyses and reports 1887-95; staff, wages, work study and welfare 1899-1928, 1877-1937: time books, wages sheets, work study labour analysis sheets, sick fund accounts, 1892-1936; savings bank ledgers and cash books 1908-37, 1928-31, 1914-18, 1917-22; house magazine 1922-70; material on the History of Xylonite and the company 1865-1981: early notes, exhibition prizes, correspondence, legal papers, press cuttings, published account 'Short History of British Xylonite 1877-1902', further notes for history 1877-1952, 1962, Queens Award to Industry 1966, dissolution of British Xylonite 1965, centenary celebration 1977, threatened closure of Brantham 1981; publications 1922-1970; photographic material 1970-1977; miscellanea 1905-1945.

J433: microfilm of Board minutes, 1877-1923.

Further records are held at:
[BXL Plastics, Buchanan House 3 St James's Square, London SW1Y 4JS:
Board minutes 1903-19, organisation circulars 1954-64; annual reports and accounts 1919-38; catalogues 1928-39; publicity material, house magazine, correspondence and photographs, miscellanea - these now appear to have been added to SRO].

Hackney Archives Department, Rose Lipman Library, De Beavoir Rd, London N 1, ref. D/B/XYL:
Corporate records: directors minutes, 1877-1925; general meeting minutes 1884-1932; corporate agreements 1877-1917; share holders register, ledgers and share certificates books, records of dividends; directors registers, balance sheets and accounts; capital reorganisation papers 1930, debenture documents and correspondence 1880-1911, interest accounts 1933-8, annual reports and accounts 1878-1959, agents ledger 1910-13, plant books, trade-mark papers 1877-1917, staff papers 1877-1917, factory sales 1896-9, property papers 1877-1917; papers of British Tortelloid: minutes 1932-8; British Xylonite (Australia) Pty Ltd 1931-1950; British Xylonite Company (Canada) Ltd: annual accounts 1922-39; BX New York Inc: 1914-27; BX Nurnberg GmbH, 1908-14; BX Wien GmbH, 1908-14; Cascelloid Ltd: minutes and accounts, 1931-50; Homerton Manufacturing Co Ltd, 1877-9; Paper Drying Co Ltd, 1894-1910; Parkesine Company Ltd, history report 1919.

The Science Museum, ref. ARCHIVES:BXL.
Vestry House Museum, Walthamstow, ref. W24.5 XYL: product catalogue, printed material, photograph and artefacts.

See also: Richmond and Stockford, (267)
Merriman, *Pioneering in Plastics* (1976)

ICI Paints Division, Stowmarket

The ICI Paints Division was established following the merger of four companies (Nobel Industries Ltd, Brunner, Mond & Company Ltd, United Alkali Company Ltd and British Dyestuffs Corporation Ltd) to form ICI in the autumn of 1926. The Stowmarket business had been founded in 1863 by the Prentice family and registered as the Patent Safety Gun

Cotton Company Ltd. After a serious explosion in 1871, killing 24 (including two of the Prentice family) and injuring 75, the factory was rebuilt in 1873-74 and the company renamed the Stowmarket Guncotton Company. The Prentice family sold out in 1880 to the Explosives Company, which had works at Pembrey, South Wales. Renamed the New Explosives Company in 1885, the Stowmarket site was extended the following year. In 1887, following the setting up of the Nobel-Dynamite Trust to restrict and control the international explosives industry, an agreement was entered into with the New Explosives Company (Nobel's key competitor in the UK) and the Pembrey factory closed. The Stowmarket factory remained in production - a new cordite factory was completed in 1898 - and after the agreement expired in 1907, Nobels Explosives Company acquired full control of the works, an event which was carefully concealed from the British government so that the company received a separate quota from the High Explosives Trade Association; it was always referred to as 'X Company' in Nobel's records. During the 1914-18 war, the factory made cordite, guncotton and cellulose syrup for aircraft 'dopes'. The workforce reached over 3,000, with women brought in from Ipswich and Bury St Edmunds. After the war, all explosives production was transferred to Ardeer, in Scotland, and Stowmarket concentrated on industrial products.

The company began the production of nitro-cellulose for industrial purposes (varnish making and film for waterproofing) in 1907. A small research labororatory was set up and, by 1912, a catalogue showing a range of nitro-cellulose products was issued. After the war new products such as plastic wood were launched, but the main focus was the development of lacquers, enamels (sold under the brand name 'Necol') and cellulose finishes to meet the potential demand from the motor industry. In 1922 the company was renamed Necol Industrial Collodians. Initially the business was lossmaking, and on 1 January 1926 the assets of Necol and Nobel's Birmingham subsidiary, Frederick Crane Chemical Company Ltd, were transferred to a new company, Nobel Chemical Finishes Ltd (in which Nobel Industries held 51 per cent of the capital and du Pont 49 per cent). After the formation of ICI, the Stowmarket factory continued to concentrate on the production of nitrocellulose varnish and paints for the motor industry and decorating trade (mostly sold under the 'Belco' or 'Dulux' brand names). During the Second World War production again centred on the war effort. By 1946, the ICI Paints Division comprised six factories. Slough (the headquarters) and Stowmarket became the focus of the Division's post-war rationalisation and expansion. A disused silk works (built on the site of the original guncotton factory) was purchased. The works were further extended and modernised throughout the 1960s and 1970s.

Records deposited at SRO (I) HC411

Seventy-four records, including typescript notes on the history of the Paints Division, press cuttings and company brochures.

Minutes, 1929-32 (Works Council Meetings, Nobel Chemical Finishes Ltd); Register of employees, c.1883-1974 (including women from 1915);

Financial records: wages, c.1913-38; departmental summaries of wages, New Explosives Co., 1921-34; file sundry accounts, 1938; 'cost report' book, Nobel Chemical Finishes, 1937-38; 'on cost allocation table' book, 1936-38.

Photographs, c.1871-1970, including those relating to the 1871 explosion. Miscellaneous, including pamphlets relating to pension and profit-sharing schemes, works council and works rules. File of newspaper cuttings.

See also:
W.J. Reader, *Imperial Chemical Industries: A History:*
Volume 1, The Forerunners 1870-1926 (1970).
Volume 11, The First Quarter-Century 1926-1952 (1975)

Kirby-Warrick Pharmaceuticals Ltd, Mildenhall

Dr E.A.Kirby established a laboratory in 1866 in Newman Street, London to prepare medicines. The company H. & T. Kirby Ltd was incorporated in 1884 to take over the business which had been established by Dr E.A. Kirby, for £80,000. In 1894 H. E. Kirby became general manager of Soden Mineral Produce Ltd, acquiring the business on its liquidation in 1894. In 1913 the business moved to Newman House, Willesden Green, London. In the 1960s in search of space for expansion the company moved to Mildenhall. In 1979 the company was taken over by Schering Corporation of USA, adopting the current name in 1980.

Records with the company at Mildenhall, Suffolk, IP28 7AX:
Share transfer certificates 1952; debenture trust deed 1921; memo and articles of association 1884, 1975, 1979; annual reports and accounts 1890, 1893, 107-50; balance sheets 1891-2; war loan papers 1925; debt papers 1937; agreement for sale of Cole and Co patent medicine business 1895; supply agreements 1890-95; pocket pharmacopoeia 1902; advertising ledgers 1884, 1900-50s; medicine case c1910; labels, 1900-54; price lists 1900-60s; samples and boxes n.d. 1904-50; formulae books 1882-1969; packaging examples 1920-72; order book 1879-80; plant examination 1972-4; managers agreement 1892; Kirby

family wills estates duty and papers 1889-1908.

See also: Richmond and Stockford, (486)

Norsk Hydro Fertilisers Group
(Fertiliser companies formerly owned by Fisons plc)

Fisons was one of the largest companies in Ipswich. For most of its history the manufacture of fertilisers and pharmaceuticals was concentrated at this site. However, the history of this company is complex. It grew, largely by acquisition, from a strong local base to become one of the major pharmaceutical and agricultural chemical companies. Its origins stretch back to 1808 when James Fison of Thetford set up as a maltster and seed and fertiliser importer, but little is known of this period. Fisons, as fertiliser manufacturers, originated in 1843 from the fertiliser business of Edward Packard. Originally a chemist he began to make fertiliser from bones before producing superphosphates (originally using local deposits of phosphates) at Snape. In 1849 he acquired land from Ransomes to build the first complete acid and superphosphate factory in the UK. The firm was incorporated in 1895 as Edward Packard and Company. with £100,000 capital. In 1919 he bought the business of James Fison of Thetford and changed the name to Packard & James Fison (Thetford) Ltd. Some decline in business led the company to seek rationalisation through amalgamation - with Joseph Fison & Co. (dates from 1847) and Prentice Bros (1856) to form Fison, Packard & Prentice Ltd in 1929. Over the next 15 years it acquired 32 existing companies (mostly with established local markets) and registered five new ones. The company thereby gained national markets but kept company names for local distribution to retain goodwill.

In 1934 they set up National Fertilisers Ltd (with the Imperial Smelting Corporation) and extended superphosphate manufacture and sales to the west of England. In 1930 a new low cost superphosphate plant at Cliff Quay, Ipswich was opened - the first completely mechanised superphosphate factory in UK.

In 1942 the firm adopted the name Fisons. By this time the group had four divisions:
1. Home region - East Anglia and South East, served by Fisons and direct subsidiaries.
2. Humber region - Doughty Goole as the controlling company.
3. Northern region - Langdales and Northern Fertilisers as the main subsidiary
4. Western region- served by National Fertilisers Ltd.

From this time some local company names were phased out and more Fisons brand names were used, with national marketing.

Also in 1937 the company took a controlling interest in Genatosan Ltd. Later the company extended its interests to pharmaceuticals medicine and various chemicals, mostly by acquisition. In 1955 the company was split into five divisions: fertilisers, agricultural chemicals, industrial and phamaceutical chemicals, ethical pharmaceuticals and proprietory medicines. The company's role in the chemical fertiliser market (together with ICI, Potash Ltd and British Basic Slag) was investigated by the Monopolies Commission in 1959 [PP. 1958/9]. The fertiliser interests of Fison were sold to Norsk Hydro in 1982 and Fisons concentrated on pharmaceuticals and fine chemicals. In 1995 the company was sold to Rhone-Poulenc Rorer Inc and renamed Rhone-Poulenc Rorer Ltd.

Records deposited at SRO (I) HC 434:
For subsidiary limited Companies still operating in 1982:

Agricultural and Lime Company Ltd
Anglo-Continental Guano
Chemical Union
Alfred Coe
John G. Cunningham
De Pass Fertilisers
Fisons
Fison Packard & Prentice
James Fison & Son
Gazyme
Ichthalmic Guano
Ipswich Printing Works
Johnson & Darling
George Johnson
Langdales Chemical Manure
Langdales & Northern Fertilisers
Lime Suppliers
J & W Maxwells
Martyjohn Mechanical Spreaders
Northern Fertilisers
North of England Chemical works

Edward Packard

Packard & James Fison (Thetford)

Prentice Brothers

Thomas Owen & Son

Thomas and Company

Various records are listed and arranged by subject and not by company; the records of the constituent companies are therefore uneven. There are 375 items listed:

Minute books, registers of debentures, registers of directors, copies of annual returns, register of transfers, of seals, certificates of incorporation, annual reports and accounts, articles of association, miscellaneous, photos, prices lists, factory valuations and inventories, insurance valuations, advertising materials.

Further items, 376-406, from non-Fisons companies.

SRO (I) HD 1648/23:

Copy of Profile magazine produced by Fisons, with article '50 years of going public'.

SRO (I) HD 1652:

Papers of Mr E.D. Wiggins, of Fisons, including type written text of draft history of company plus papers relating to it; illustrations for history of constituent companies including a chart showing dates of origin and absorption of all 76 companies from 1843 to c1945; photos and sundry papers, including some referring to Levington research station.

In aggregate these provide a major source for business history.

Other records:

Principally these are held by Rhone-Poulenc Rorer Ltd. Enquiries to Rhone-Poulenc Rorer House, 50, Kings Hill Avenue, Kings Hill, West Malling ME19 4AH.

Records at London Metropolitan Archives B/WHF/1-245:

Fisons Chemicals (export) Ltd, memorandum and articles of association 1951; correspondence, circulars and press cutting 1948-1951.

At History of Advertising Trust, HAT House, 12 Raveningham Centre, Norwich NR14 6NU:

Guardbooks of advertising material 1942, 1955-63.

Suffolk Chemical Company, Ipswich
Industrial chemicals

The Suffolk Chemical Company was based at Cliff Quay, Ipswich. It distilled industrial alcohol (methylated spirits), importing molasses from the West Indies, Cuba, Egypt and the Phillipines, subsequently also using supplies from the factories of the British Sugar Company. In 1928 the business became a subsidiary of Reckitt & Sons of Hull (from 1938, Reckitt & Colman). Industrial alcohol provided the base for some of Reckitt's products, such as polishes, although some products were also made under the Suffolk Chemical Company's name. Until 1939 coasting steamers transported the spirit direct from the Ipswich factory to Hull. Reckitts closed the company in 1958 when new, cheaper methods of producing industrial alcohol from petroleum were developed.

Records held by Reckitt Benckiser: enquiries to the Archivist, Dansom Lane, Hull HU8 7DS. Annual report 1933; nominal ledger 1942-58; Journal (ledger) 1957.

See also: Reckitt & Colman Magazine (Reckitt Edition), Spring 1953.

ENGINEERING

Atco-Qualcast Ltd, Stowmarket
Lawn mower manufacturers

The original firm was founded by Louis John Tibbenham (b. 1879) as Suffolk Iron Founders in 1913, when he took over the local firm of Woods and Co which had gone into liquidation. Tibbenham had served as an apprentice with Ransomes in Ipswich and subsequently worked for Clayton and Shuttleworth and Ruston and Hornsby of Lincoln before returning to Suffolk. Suffolk Iron Founders appears to have gone into liquidation shortly after the First World War and was re-established in 1920 as Suffolk Iron Founders (1920) Ltd. making castings for various local businesses and subsequently various consumer goods from cast iron like mangles, mincers and sports equipment and a simple hand mower. The firm also developed oxy-acetylene welding equipment (and Tibbenham produced more than one technical book on the process) and were particularly well known for bronze welding from the 1920s, making 'Sifbronze' rods and fluxes. There was a high export orientation in the inter-war years. In 1933 a Mr Kaufmann had acquired a share in the business and became responsible for marketing. During the Second World War the firm made bomb trolleys for the RAF. The first petrol motor powered mowers were produced in the 1950s, the 'Suffolk Punch' model being made from 1954. Tibbenham retired in 1955 and Kaufmann took over the business. In 1958 it joined the Derby based Qualcast group and this in turn merged with Birmetals (of Birmingham) to form the Birmid Qualcast Group in 1967. Motor mowers were by this time a major part of the business; all parts were made on the Stowmarket site including 100,000 engines each year. In 1988 Blue Circle Industries took over Birmid, the Derby site was closed and all mower manufacture moved to Stowmarket in 1991. [Blue Circle owned a variety of businesses including Qualcast ceramics. Suffolk Iron Founders was now renamed as Suffolk Lawn Mowers. The name Atco came from a company owned by Charles H. Pugh.] The mower works was acquired in a management buyout in 1992; this in turn was sold to Robert Bosch in 1995. The company is still trading. The welding business was taken over in a separate management buyout (to become 'Sifbronze') in 1993.

Records are privately held by: Mr P. Tibbenham, Sifbronze, Prentice Road, Stowmarket: Unpublished autobiography by Louis John Tibbenham; his original apprentice agreement with Ransomes, Sims and Jefferies, 1894, employment agreement with Rustons and Hornsbys, Lincoln; papers of Woods and Co.; trade agreements, accounts, terms of employment; copies of trade journals and other publications with reference to business; miscellaneous technical correspondence 1920-1939, miscellaneous correspondence with suppliers and customers, 1914-1951; copies of extracts from Stowmarket Chronicle (January 1964); maps, photographs, miscellaneous memorabilia.

A serialised account of Louis John Tibbenham's work appeared in the *Stowmarket Chronicle*, January 1964.

Robert Boby Ltd, St. Andrews St, Bury St Edmunds
Agricultural and malting engineering

The machine shop at the Bury St Edmunds engineers, Robert Boby, 1924.

The earliest record of this business was of an ironmonger at 7 Meat Market (later Cornhill) Bury St Edmunds, in 1843. In 1851 Robert Boby was contracted to install gas lighting in St James Chapel. In 1855 Boby with Thomas Cooper Bridgman took out a patent for an improvement in corn dressing and winnowing machines (in effect a self cleaning screen). The firm then became known for agricultural machines and malting equipment. Robert Boby died in 1886; his business was taken over by his nephew C.E.

Munford (his only son was said not to be interested in the business; he also had four daughters). The business was sold to a new company and incorporated in January 1898 as 'Robert Boby Ltd.' with a share capital of £10,000. In the First World War it had contracts with Vickers for armaments. In 1918 Vickers took a share and from 1919 Bobys effectively became a subsidiary of Vickers though this company took all share capital only from 1930 (in the Bury records the date is given as 1927). However, despite continued growth and diversification in production (agricultural equipment had a very difficult time in the early 1930s), the firm was constantly in financial difficulties and was propped up by the parent company. Attempts were made to sell Bobys in 1926/7 and 1935 but without success. Demand in World War II and subsequently helped the business. Share capital reached £500,000 in 1951. The company closed in 1971

Records deposited at SRO (B) HC 537, E5/2/6.1 and K 770
Order Books, annually 1866-1909 with analyses of number and destination of different products sold each year; product technical drawings, 1927-45; photograph.
The records are limited but provide a useful picture of sales and markets. They are held in a separate store and normally twenty-four hours notice is required to see them.

Other records in Cambridge University Library as part of the Vickers Archive:
Documents 605 and 771 on the history of the firm; Minute Books 1898-1962 as documents 1212 to 1218; production records 1939-45 (717); quarterly reports 1946-62 (220-283).

Part of the Bury St Edmunds factory was moved to the Museum of East Anglian Life, Stowmarket where, as the Boby Building, it houses a permanent display of the company's objects. A collection of catalogues is held in the Museum library.

See also *Guide, 9* This additionally lists: annual a/c 1948-64, quarterly a/c 1946-62, [not located]

John Chambers Ltd, Lowestoft
Shipbuilders and marine engineers

The business was founded by John Chambers and Charles Page in 1877. It became the first local shipyard to build a steam drifter, the Consolation, launched in 1879.

Records deposited at SRO (L) Ac no 18:
Memoranda and articles of association 1913; day book 1913-27; accounts 1913-19 (6 vols); inventory and valuation of properties 1925.

Cocksedge and Co. Ltd, Ipswich
Structural engineering

In 1879 James Cocksedge (previously a partner in the firm of Woods, Cocksedge & Company, of the Suffolk Iron Works) moved from Stowmarket and set up a small engineering works, employing about 12 people, to take on any general engineering work. In 1887 Cocksedge died. His sons Edmund and Arthur, took over and subsequently extended the business into structural engineering. In 1900 the business moved to new premises in Rapier St, and in 1925 became a private limited company. Structural engineering work included farm buildings, stands at Newmarket and sports ground throughout the country, bridges, Fisons fertiliser factory, and numerous buildings for Butlin's holiday camps. The firm also maintained a general engineeering side, making various chaff cutting machines, mostly for export, and industrial scales (these included scales for race course weighing rooms). The latter enterprise was sold as a separate business in 1936. The mechanical engineering was applied to a wide range of industrial and agricultural uses, including sugar beet slicing; the company also supplied beet conveyors and complete diffusion batteries. During the war years, in common with many other engineering works, the business diversified into defence supply making air raid shelters, Bailey bridges, gun emplacements, components for tanks and a complete DDT factory. The foundry was closed after the war and greater emphasis was placed on the manufacture of special purpose plant, especially for the sugar industry, involving worldwide exports. The company also secured large admiralty contracts besides that for the Goonhilly No 2 Satellite Tracking Station. By the early 1950s the firm was employing around 550. It continued to flourish until the 1970s, but the growing use of pre-cast concrete steadily diminished the demand for structural steel. The workforce was cut to 180 but receivers were called in during September 1985.

Records deposited at SRO (I) HC 457:
Apprentice indentures (from 1803), partnerships, building valuations (1930s), memoranda and articles of association, (1955); deeds and agreements, 1803-1979; financial records 1881-1957; machinery plant and stock 1887, 1900-33; miscellaneous including papers relating to history of the company, 1810-1979, cuttings, genealogical

papers, 1783-1957; photographs and portraits, c1870-1979.

Eastern Coach Works Ltd, Lowestoft
Bus and coach bodybuilders

Ernest Hutchinson founded United Automobile Services Ltd in 1912, initially providing bus services in the Lowestoft area and then around Bishop Auckland, County Durham. In August 1914, the United fleet comprised twenty-seven vehicles; by 1919 this had increased to sixty-four, and by 1928 to over 600, operating throughout Suffolk, Norfolk, Lincolnshire, County Durham, Yorkshire and Northumberland. From 1919 the company began converting ex-army vehicles and two years later built its first new coach bodies. In 1925 the bodybuilding activities were extended, with complete buses and coaches supplied to other operators. By 1922 the company employed a workforce of around 300.

In 1929 Tilling and British Automobile Traction Ltd and the LNER took joint control and two years later the company merged with Eastern Counties Road Car Company Ltd, Ipswich, Ortona Motor Company Ltd, Cambridge, and Peterborough Electric Traction Company Ltd, to form Eastern Counties Omnibus Company. Between 1931 and 1936 nearly 1,700 bus and coach bodies were built for many of the larger operators throughout the country. During this time a manufacturing partnership with the chassis-building division of Bristol Tramways & Carriage Company was established which lasted until 1983. In 1940 the Lowestoft factory was closed (although partially reopened later in the year) and production moved to Irthlingborough in Northamptonshire, Lowestoft becoming fully operational again at the end of 1944.

In 1942 control of the company passed to Tilling Motor Services Ltd. Six years later it came under the umbrella of the British Transport Commission, with production subsequently limited to other nationalised operators. In 1965 Leyland Motors Ltd took a 25 per cent share in the company, increased four years later to 50 per cent with the formation of the National Bus Company (a development which again enabled the production of bodies for non-nationalised operators); full control was achieved in 1982, Eastern Coach Works becoming a subsidiary of Bus Manufacturing Ltd. Recession in the bus manufacturing industry in the early 1980s saw the workforce reduced by half to just over 400. In 1986 the government ordered the sale of Leyland Bus which was purchased by a management consortium. Eastern Coach Works was subsequently closed.

Records deposited at SRO (L) Ac no 174:

Typescript company history; memoranda and articles of association 1931-75, The Tilling Association Ltd 1942, 1957; board and shareholders attendance books 1936-70 (2 vols); executive committee minutes 1965-70; management meeting minutes 1969-70; annual reports and statements of account 1937-75 (44 docs); Tilling Group schedule of accounts 1953-64; Transport Holding Co statements of account 1965-67; capitalisation 1953; impersonal ledgers 1936-70 (5); nominal ledgers 1936-52 (3); nominal and impersonal ledger 1970; journals 1936-78 (7); sales journals 1942-62 (13); cash books 1944-62 (6); payments cash books 1948-50 (5); patents 1942-53; design agreements 1942-52; product specifications 1954-70; vehicle record books 1945-72; brochures 1986; photographs of products c1932-72; staff welfare society 1938-77 (AGM minutes, balance sheet, accounts); staff photographs 1953; endowment fund, report and statement of accounts 1943-69; property deeds 1936-75 (includes site plan 1946).

See also: Maurice Doggett, *Eastern Coach Works: a history of the coachbuilding activities at Lowestoft 1919-1946*, Vol 1 (1987)

Maurice Doggett and Alan Townsin, *Eastern Coach Works*, 1946-1965 (1993)

Duncan Robert and John Senior, *Eastern Coach Works of Lowestoft: a retrospect* (1995).

Elliott & Garrood Ltd, Beccles
Marine engineering

The business of Elliott & Garrood was founded by William Elliott (1838-1908) c1868. Apprenticed to engineers, Watts & Riches, by the 1870s he was established in Blyburghgate Street, Beccles, as a general engineer. His first significant invention, a steam driven power unit for farmers (known as the 'farmers boy') provided the prototype for his renowned patent steam 'Beccles capstan' for fishing boats, first advertised in 1884. That year, Elliott entered into partnership with William Garrood, an agricultural engineer from Wheatacre, near Haddiscoe, whose business acumen complemented Elliott's inventive ability. The business expanded rapidly. Between 1885-94 200 capstans were fitted to fishing vessels; in 1897, a triple expansion engine - the 'monkey triple' - was developed; a compound marine engine, steam line hauler, steam donkey pumps, trawl winch and rope coilers followed. Branches were opened at Lowestoft, Great Yarmouth, Brixham, Newlyn, Buckie and Fraserburgh, and agencies established in Holland, Germany and Norway.

In 1897, Elliott & Garrood was registered as a private limited company with a capital of £60,000, with William Elliott (chairman), William Garrood (deputy chairman) and their sons, William Jacob and Alexander Elliott and William George and Frederick Garrood, as directors. The business remained a family firm for three generations until its take-over in 1959 by A. King & Sons of Norwich. Within two years it was merged into the Metropole Group of companies. The discovery of North Sea gas led to rapid expansion and a range of valves, adapted for chemical, plastic and mining industries, were developed and manufactured at Beccles. In 1970, the firm was acquired by the Dobson Park Group of Nottingham. Two years later the marine interests were relocated to premises in Suffolk Road, Lowestoft, before moving to a new site at Riverside Road, Gorleston where Whittacker launch and recovery capsules were made and distributed. The Beccles industrial valve interests were sold (1972) to Sir W.H.Bailey & Co. of Manchester (part of the Imperial Metal Industries group). The company, restyled IM Bailey Valves, amalgamated with Samuel Birkett Limited in 1981 to become IM Bailey Birkett. The Beccles site was closed in November of that year.

Records deposited at SRO (L) Ac nos 40; 523:
Memoranda and articles of association 1897; directors' meeting agenda book 1898-1901; directors' report, profit and loss account and balance sheets, 1818, 1938, 1947-57; shareholdings (2 items); private ledgers 1923-29, 1938-46; private cash book 1918-35, 1936-62; summary of accounts 1890-1897; ledgers (general) 1897-1917; customers' ledger 1878-95, 1900-55; customers' accounts 1917-c1958; bought ledgers Nos 4-7, 10-12, 1909-34, 1941-51, 1955-60; cash ledger 1930-59; cash payments account book 1949-55; rents cash book 1915-59; allotments rent account book 1936-59; bank book 1899-1900; works ledgers 1901-59; order books 1910-11, 1932-57; capstan and boiler stock registers 1896-1911; capstan indices 1884-1930, including Scottish 1893-1908, 1925-37, Continental 1894-1907, English 1923-24; capstan registers 1892-52; price and promotional material c1922-56; goods inwards book; inventory and valuation 1920, 1941; technical drawings and specifications, including microfilm of plans and drawings 1925-67; book of rough plans of capstans and boilers 1888-90; steam capstan plans (nd); publicity material 1969 (2 items).
File of press cuttings (Beccles firms)

See also: Christopher R. Elliott, 'The Fisherman's Friend', *East Coast Digest*, Vol 3, 1974, No 1.

W.J. Ford & Sons, West Row, Mildenhall
Agricultural engineering

Records deposited at SRO (B): HC 556:

Ledgers: repairs 1922-25, 1937-38, 1942-43, 1972-87; purchases 1932-45, 1950-55; outline accounts 1926-32; receipts 1891-1937; threshing receipts 1904-39; bought 1926-29; day books 1929-36; sales 1937-39 (35 volumes).

Richard Garrett Engineering Ltd, Leiston
Agricultural engineering

6 RICHARD GARRETT É HIJOS, Leiston Works, Suffolk, Inglaterra.

RICHARD GARRETT É HIJOS.

MÁQUINA DE VAPOR LOCOMÓVIL DE UN CILINDRO,

Con regulador de muelles laminados patente de Garrett y aparato de subir y bajar la chimenea.

The Leiston engineers, Richard Garrett & Sons, exported machinery and engines worldwide. This advert is from the firm's late nineteenth-century Spanish catalogue.

The firm originated in 1778 when Richard Garrett moved to Leiston from Woodbridge - he opened a blacksmith shop and forge. His son, also Richard, took over in 1805; a third Richard was born in 1807 and was in charge by 1836. The firm remained in family partnership until 1897 when it was incorporated as 'Richard Garrett and Sons Ltd'. (His third son founded a similar business in Magdeburg.) This was the period of most rapid growth - the firm had a peak of 2000 employees in 1913. The main business was in exports of agricultural engineering, though military orders were important in the 1914-1918 war. However, a financial crisis followed because of the repudiation of Russian debt and presumably the drying up of trade in much of continental Europe. The firm, in common with many others in this industry, began a period of decline. An amalgamation of 11 companies was forced (these included Aveling and Porter, Burrells and others) as 'Agricultural and General Engineers' in 1920, operating from Aldwych House. This was an unsuccessful venture because of company rivalries. The receiver was called in 1931, and the constituent companies sold separately. Garretts was bought by Beyer Peacock and Co. Ltd of Gorton, Manchester and renamed Richard Garrett Engineering Ltd. In 1976 the equity of Beyer was bought by NCI (a construction company based in Saudi Arabia); Garretts was by that time the major part of the business. In 1980 Garretts was sold to Nicol Industries Ltd who subsequently disposed of the business in five parts. One of the Leiston sites, the Station works, continued to operate until 1985 when it was closed. (The Long Shop museum was set up on one of old sites in Leiston.)

Records deposited at SRO (I) HC 30:
This is one of the most extensive company holdings in Ipswich (records deposited 1973-1982); it has a catalogue file to itself, in which entries alone cover 204 pages.
The records concentrate on trading, technical and manufacturing of agricultural and general engineering from 1890s to 1932 (insolvency). Most of the records (on pp 52-186 of the file HC30) are technical rather than commercial in nature, including several thousand drawings (about 75 per cent of the original total), and refer to the period before 1932. Many corporate and administrative records appear to have been destroyed during World War II. Copies of drawings are available on request from SRO (I).

Memoranda and articles of association 1897, directors attendance book 1857-1980, ledger, 1845-1924, day books 1887-1933, bill books 1881-1929, register of charitable donations 1860-1914, agricultural machinery order books 1895-1928, (from 1908 a distinction is made between home and export sales), thresher order books, 1920-1933, costing and prices books 1860-1903, calculations 1898-1931, stock books 1913-31, register of engines, 1866-1951, engine reference notebooks 1864-1907, engine specifications and testing records 1908-1930, monthly output summaries 1903-28, memoranda books re products and overseas customers, spec. technical drawings, register of castings, forgings etc. sketch book 1909-49, testing records, log sheets, product files, patents 1842-74, journeymen ledgers 1869-1915, wages and salaries books 1888-1936, valuation of buildings 1866, inventories 1877-1924, canteen book 1921-5, a/c housing repairs 1919-21, catalogues from 1859.

Some records of Beyer Peacock are held in Greater Manchester Museum of Science and Industry (a list of material is in SRO(I)).

Artefacts and objects are displayed in the Long Shop Museum , Leiston.

See also: R.A.Whitehead, *Garretts of Leiston* (1964)
R.A.Whitehead, *Garretts 200. A bicentenary history of Garretts of Leiston, 1778-1978* (1978). Also by the same author: *Garrett Diesel Tractors* (1994); *Garrett Wagons* (in three parts, 1994-6); *Garrett Tractors and Ploughing Engines* (1996); *The beloved coast and the Suffolk sandlings* (1991) pp. 159-172 for details of Long Shop Museum.
H.T. Cadbury-Brown and J. Metcalfe, *The Long Shop, Richard Garrett works, Leiston*, a report for the Suffolk Preservation Society, (1977).
V.B. Redstone *The Suffolk Garretts* (1916)

Ransomes plc (now Textron), Ipswich
Agricultural engineering

The company was known as Ransomes, Sims and Jefferies from incorporation in 1884 to 1989. The company was founded in 1789 in Ipswich by Robert Ransome a Quaker from north Norfolk, who had earlier operated in Norwich. The firm was best known for plough making. In 1785 Ransome patented a method of tempering cast iron plough shares and later patented a 'chilling' method for the same and, in 1808, for interchangeable plough parts. It was clearly an innovative business. The company was the first to produce gas for lighting in Ipswich, in 1817, pre-dating the Ipswich Gas Light Company by four years. It was also the first in the town to install a steam engine, in 1831. The company name changed subsequently on several occasions before incorporation as a private limited company, 'Ransomes, Sims and Jefferies Ltd' in 1884. In 1911 it became a public company.

The original business was ploughs and other farm equipment and machinery, including threshing machines and portable steam engines. The company built up an international reputation for these products and had extensive overseas markets before the end of the nineteenth century. In 1832 the company began to make grass cutting machines (another 'first' though the device was invented by Edwin Budding in Stroud) and subsequently produced also railway components, a steamship, electric vehicles, amusement machines and the mechanism for the astronomical equipment in the Greenwich observatory. In 1871 the company made to order four steam powered road going vehicles for the Indian government; 1902 saw the first petrol driven lawn mower and in the following year an early but unsuccessful petrol farm tractor. During the First World War they made aeroplanes which went into service, and with the return to peace, more lawn mowers, electric vehicles and trolley buses. However, major markets in Russia (this had been the largest export outlet before 1914) and Latin America had been largely lost, the first following the social and economic effects of the 1917 revolution, the second because of inroads from United States. In the Second World War they once again made supplies for the armed forces and set up a special school to train newly recruited women war workers in engineering skills. After the war they extended the electric vehicle side of the business to include fork lift trucks. In the longer term the company became more specialised, however. The industrial engineering and railway business had been separated to 'Ransomes and Rapier Ltd' [q.v.] as early as 1869. Gradually other businesses were sold in the face of competition: electric vehicles in 1980, farm machinery in 1987, leaving grass cutting machinery as the major part of the business. In 1989 the company changed its name to Ransomes plc. The company was taken over by the Textron group of USA in 1998 and continues to trade concentrating on commercial grass care equipment.

The records for this company constitute one of the most detailed for any agricultural engineering firm in the country. Although the greater part are located outside the county they provide a most detailed source for Suffolk business history.

Major records at the Rural History Centre and Museum of English Rural Life, University of Reading:
These are extremely extensive and excellently well catalogued, all with the prefix, TR RAN/. A full survey of this holding was published in 1975: D.R.Grace and D.C. Phillips, *Ransomes of Ipswich, A History of the Firm and Guide to its records* (Institute of Agricultural History, 1975). Most of the records refer to the nineteenth century. The catalogue in the archives in Reading is extremely detailed and carefully annotated and provides an

excellent guide and finding aid.

The deposit includes: Accounts, private ledgers 1884-1944, cost accounts, including wages and salaries for the period 1871-1940, financial statements and branch accounts, for Ipswich, 1916-1947 and Odessa, 1892-1919; administrative and commercial records, from 1884, minutes general administrative and commercial records, labour records from 1835 and records relating to premises, materials, branches (principally between 1846 and 1918); commercial records, including order books, sales analyses (variously from 1866 to 1950), prices records, export books for Peru, Columbia, Roumania and Russia, agencies books for England, Wales, Scotland and Ireland, records of travelling (1897, 1929, 1930, 1961), miscellaneous commercial records 1845-1969, 1906-1961; general correspondence, letter book 1875-1955; legal records of companies and businesses from 1809, including partnership agreements, records of registered companies, external agreements, patents and trade marks; drawings, including steam engines, threshers with indexes, including those for Ruston and Hornsby; technical records of experiments and trials, technical reference records, patents and technical specifications, photographs; manufacturing and production (between 1846 and 1948), including engine registers, traction engine registers, steam wagon registers, and of corn mills, threshing machinery, ploughs, electric vehicles, manufacturing working papers, parts, repairs and outwork records; publication, promotion and advertising from 1800, including general publications, trade catalogues, posters, house journals, advertising records, printing proofs and artwork; internal photographic records; shows and exhibitions, certificates, awards and general records; social and personal records, including internal histories, events societies and organisations, records of products, press cuttings and personal records.

All of these are fully itemised in part 2 of Grace and Phillips, pp. 29-64, which itself presents only a summary of the full catalogue.

Other records:
The Company:
From 1793 including directors' minutes from 1884, directors' private memoranda 1892-1965, financial statements 1851-80, memoranda books (3) 1890s-1920s, bad debt notebooks 1878-1927, order books 1852-84, James Ransomes' sketch book of plough design early 19th C pattern books (2) 1849-1918, wages book (2) 1859-71, 1900-10, salaries books (2) 1863-86, 1908-26 fines a/c books 1883-1917, list of workmen 1793-1841, abstract of apprentice indentures 1840-78. Public relations literature, leaflets, photographs, press cuttings; register of lawn mowers manufactured since 1832.

Also records of Johnson (Engineering) Ltd. 1941-68 (minute books, register of members, share certificates etc.) and similar for Johnson (Implements) Scotland Ltd.

Catchpole Engineering Co. Ltd. (Directors and general meeting minutes, 1947-91, share registers, articles of association 1947, Company agreements, pension arrangements.)

Lincs Archives (Ruston and Hornsby):
Grantham branch cash book 1930-7 and salaries book 1930-7

Records at SRO (I):
Photographs and printed materials about Ipswich trolley and motor buses

See also: *Guide, vol. 9.*(973) and Richmond and Stockford, 467

A. Beaumont, *Ransomes Steam engines: an illustrated history* (Newton Abbot, 1972)

C. and M. Weaver, *Ransomes, 1789-1989. 200 years of excellence* (Ipswich, 1989).

R. Munting, 'Ransomes in Russia: An English Agricultural Engineering Company's Trade with Russia to 1917', *Economic History Review*, Vol XXXI, No 2, 1978.

Ransomes & Rapier plc
Industrial engineering

The firm was established in 1869 by Ransomes, Sims and Jefferies, and took over industrial engineering and railway manufacture from the parent company in that year; it was incorporated in 1896. Taking advantage of the growing international market for railways the new company made equipment such as points and buffers as well as gang trolleys and cranes. In 1874 they also built the first steam engine to be used in China, on the Shanghai to Woosong line. The firm developed large breakdown cranes for railways and, in the 1920s, the first road going mobile crane. Other products for which the company became well known were mechanical excavators and water control systems and sluice gates, which were used in irrigation schemes world wide. The company developed in general engineering with large export markets. However, in the 1960s it faced the first of several setbacks as world demand for its products contracted. Closure was threatened, with the loss of all 780 jobs, in 1972, though this was successfully resisted; the factory was bought by the Central and Sherwood engineering group, and briefly returned to profitability. Further contractions in demand followed in the 1980s with consequent job losses. In May 1987, following losses of £3.7 million in 1986, the company was bought by the Hollis Group, owned by Robert Maxwell. As losses continued to grow the holding company declared the intention to close the works in July 1987. Despite strong local resistance closure was confirmed in September. The factory closed in March 1988 and production transferred to a sister company in Bath. The building was demolished in 1993.

Records deposited at SRO (I) HB 439 and HC 427:

These are extensive records, four deposits under different accession numbers the two largest covering 147 feet and 51 feet, linear, respectively. They are not catalogued in as detailed a manner as some other but are listed in class list.

Acc. 8445: AGM minutes, 1897-1931, 1961-72; Board minutes, 1896-1972, shareholders register, 1896-1958; annual export balance sheets, 1896-1933; plant and machinery records, 1869-1943; superannuation records, salaries, accident records; Directors' correspondence, patents drawings.

Acc. 8479: Engineering drawings, photo albums; order abstract book. 1875-1961, publicity material, 1938-71; engineering notebook.

Acc. 8558: Plans of Waterside Works, Ipswich, 1890-20thC.

Acc. 8647: Certificate of incorporation 1896; correspondence 1877-1920s; order abstract book 1930-38; buildings and premises 1916-60, commission claim books, 1904-17, superannuation fund a/c; private journal 1946-61, cash book, 1948-73; agreements with J Ver Mehr, 1907-10.

See also: *Guide, vol. 9* (972): including certificate of association 1896, board minutes 1896-1972, etc. as above plus, additionally: papers relating to Shanghai-Woosung railway 1873-5.

R.S. Lewis, *Eighty years of enterprise, 1869-1949, being the intimate story of the Waterside works of Ransomes and Rapier Ltd of Ipswich,* (Ipswich, 1950)

James Smyth & Sons Ltd, Peasenhall
Agricultural engineering

Smyths dates from 1792; it became a well known company based on more or less a single product, the seed drill. A Rev. J. Cooke developed a seed drill which was improved by I. A. Baldwin a farmer from Mendham. Smyth began working in a small country workshop in 1797 and was known to be making drills (which might have been improvements of Cooke's) in the early part of the nineteenth century. The firm was well established by 1808. Subsequently the market was extended to include exports throughout the world. This involved the development of specialised products including drills for ground nuts, sugar beet as well as grains, manure etc. The firm was still operating in the 1960s but ceased trading in 1968, presumably as demand for its specialised products withered.

Records deposited at SRO (I) HC23:
Shares 1908-9, 1927-31 correspondence; finance (including balance sheets for 1924-31); patents and trade marks (dating from 1843, and including French and German patents; further from 1892, 1900, 1953; correspondence with Belgium, Kenya, S. Africa, USA and others); design and publicity (general publicity, price lists for 1950, 1960s; catalogues, including some in French, 1899, 1900; instructions for use - French, German, Russian; a publicity leaflet in Russian for model 32 drill, 1960s, together with invoices for sale of spare parts for same); sales and servicing (including 67 indexed order books 1847-1968, undifferentiated by export or home sales); Peasenhall site (plans building etc.); Witham site, Essex (title deed); history of the firm (notes on the history- old newspaper cuttings; school essays); history of drill making (publications); miscellaneous (shareholders, maps).

Records at the Museum of East Anglian Rural Life, Stowmarket (enquiries to the Curator):
76D 31/1 Order Book for agricultural equipment 13/3/1867 - 31/10/1867
76.D.11/31 Miscellaneous printed matter, pamphlets, letter heads; photographs.
A small collection of objects is housed in the Boby Building.

See also *Guide, 9*: This lists some additional records, (not all of which have been located in SRO(I)): Share correspondence 1908-9, 1927-31, a/c 1924-31, a/c books including valuation 1844-8, number books (20) for customer orders, 1836-71, boxes and frames 1873-1967, horse hoes 1897-1912, steerages 1916-59, work sheets and engineering drawings patents, trade marks and related papers 1843-1939, price lists 1920-65 catalogue, photos, deeds, c1700-1859, plan 1924, sale particulars 1968, press cuttings.

The workshop of the Peasenhall engineering firm of James Smyth & Sons, c1900. The firm specialised in seed drills which were exported to many countries.

W.E.Wigg & Son, Barnby
Agricultural engineers

The business was founded in 1802 and closed in 1991. Most records have been destroyed.

Records deposited at SRO (L) Ac no 495:
Ledgers of customer's accounts, 1898-1915 (three volumes).

FOOD PROCESSING

Adnams & Co Plc, Sole Bay Brewery, Southwold
Brewing

The Sole Bay Brewery began as a brewhouse adjoining the seventeenth-century Old Swan Hotel, Southwold. Purchased in 1825 and rebuilt by William Crisp, after his death in 1844 the brewery was acquired by John Woodley of Cambridge. His nephew, William Woodley, went into partnership with Samual Gayfer of Walberswick, trading as Gayfer & Woodley. The partnership was dissolved in 1851, Gayfer continuing as sole proprietor until his death three years later. The brewery failed to sell at auction, but by 1864 was worked by Samuel Fitch. He retired in 1870 to concentrate on his mineral water and wine interests and soon after the brewery was leased by George and Ernest Adnams from Berkshire. George Adnams left the business around 1872 and Ernest went into partnership with Thomas Sergeant, trading as Adnams & Sergeant. In March 1890 Adnams & Company Limited was registered as a private limited liability company. The brewery was rebuilt and by 1897 the company had acquired twenty-three freehold and seven leasehold houses and two freehold hotels in Suffolk, Norfolk and Essex. In 1904 it acquired the business and properties of C.J. Fisher & Company of Church Street, Eye, Suffolk (founded 1874); the licensed properties of E. Rope & Company of Orford, Suffolk, in 1922; the brewery and properties of Flintham Hall & Company Limited, Aldeburgh, Suffolk, in 1924. The company name was changed to Adnams & Company Plc in 1985, at which time it employed 43 staff and operated seventy tied houses.

Records held by the company:
Directors' minutes 1897-date; general meeting minutes 1890-date; debenture holders' meeting minutes 1940; registers: directors 1897-date; members 1897-date; mortgages and bonds 1890-1908; share application book 1901-04; balance sheets and profit and loss accounts 1897-1960; ledgers: impersonal 1898-1950; nominal 1960-64; rent 1906-39; Swan Hotel 1932-48; free trade book 1948-54; brewing books 18..-1964; copper hops book 1955-64; wine and spirits: cellar book 1938-46; bottling book 1963-73; monthly production book 1905-20; brewing letterbook, R.F.B. Coling, director and partner in steam brewery, Chard, Somerset 1852-1923.

See also: Richmond and Turton, pp.37-38.

Edward Baker Ltd, Cornard Mills
Flour milling and pet foods

Edward Baker bought Cornard Mill in 1851. (His father had run the maltings of Prentice Ltd in Lavenham.) He died in 1891 and was succeeded by his son Sydney. Sydney's son Alan in turn took over in 1921 and was joined by G.B. Stannard. Alan's brothers Edward, Hugh and Kenneth joined as directors in 1922 when the company was incorporated as Edward Baker Ltd. The company was innovative in introducing steam milling in the late nineteenth century, building a special railway siding after the First World War. The firm diversified into animal feeds in the 1930s, following a Dutch example. In 1943 they bought Greens Mill, Maldon. In 1955 the firm was restructured as Edward Baker Holdings Ltd, with newly named Edward Baker Ltd and Green Bros (Maldon) as operating companies. In 1955 they set up a subsidiary company to market a bulk feed transporter, to replace carriage in sacks. Called the 'Bulkmobile', it was designed in house and produced from 1956. It was a technical success, with sales in many parts of Europe, though ultimately commercially disappointing and production was ended by 1989. From 1967 flour milling was concentrated at Maldon and animal feeds at Great Cornard. In 1984 the firm ceased animal feed manufacture and concentrated exclusively on pet foods. Five years later Edward Baker was sold to Harrisons & Crosfield plc. A new factory was opened at the Chiltern Industrial Estate, near Sudbury, the following year. The company has become one of the largest dry and semi-moist pet foods manufacturers in Europe, winning the Queen's Award for Export Achievement in 1988 and 1993.

Records deposited at SRO (B) HC 545:

This is a major resource in Bury.

Corporate records; Minute Books of Directors and AGMs 1922-49, 1949-55 and 1955-78; Company Secretary's papers (including sale of company in 1989); finance records; production records (including manuscript notes on procedures for malting barley c1888. And various papers and statistics on production 1909-1919, purchases and production 1930-1948); advertising; staff; premises and plant, covers period 1794-1960s; subsidiary companies (1956-76), (including Bulkmobile, Cornard Electronics); miscellaneous; Baker family.

See also: Hugh Baker, *The Story of Cornard Mills*, (privately published 1994)

Birds Eye Wall's Ltd, Lowestoft
Frozen foods

In November 1943 Unilever acquired from Frosted Foods Ltd (the UK frozen foods division of the American Group, General Foods) the controlling interest in Birds Eye Foods Ltd. Three years later, attracted by East Anglian agricultural produce and local fish, the company opened a factory at Great Yarmouth. In 1949 a unit was opened at Rant Score, Lowestoft, to prepare and pack fruit for the Yarmouth factory. By the summer of 1952 a unit for frozen food production was completed and the factory subsequently processed peas, stringless beans, fish and a variety of soft fruits. In 1960, with the opening of the biggest cold store in Europe, the Lowestoft labour force - initially fewer than 200 - was increased to 1,400 during the peak seasonal period. In 1981 the company merged with T. Wall & Sons Ltd (Unilever's ice cream subsidiary) to form Birds Eye Wall's Ltd, bringing all frozen food production together under one company. Two years later, with the proposed closure of the Yarmouth factory, waffle and burger production were moved to Lowestoft and in 1988 the entire vegetable repack operation was concentrated at the factory. In 1991, following an investment of £17 million, a further production unit was opened, the workforce reaching approximately 1,500. Around 15,000 tonnes annually of frozen peas and potato products were exported, through Felixstowe, to Europe (in particular Italy). In 1999 the company contracted out all pea freezing but continued the packing operation.

The Birds Eye Wall's archives are part of the Unilever archive.
Material relating to the Lowestoft factory is limited mostly to photographs and in-house magazines. Access to the collection is strictly by appointment and application must be made in writing in the first instance to the Corporate Archivist, Unilever House, Blackfriars, London, EC4P 4BQ.

See also: W.J. Reader, *Birds Eye: the Early Years* (1963)
Graham Kemp, 'The Birds Eye Story', *Frozen Foods*, 1961.

British Sugar, Hollow Road, Bury St Edmunds
Sugar processing

The United Sugar Company was incorporated in January 1925, the Bury factory opening in December of that year. (Press cuttings suggest that building was under way during 1923-4.) It had a capacity for 1,000 tons per day but began operations taking only 500 tons. The company was part of the Bury Group (which built factories also in Peterborough, Selby and Allscott in Shropshire), an Anglo-Hungarian company the major shareholder of which was Tate and Lyle, the refiners. Accordingly, unlike the rival factory in Ipswich [q.v.], the Bury factory did not refine sugar but produced only raws for refining in Liverpool or London. The rapid growth of the beet sugar industry followed the Sugar Industry (subsidy) Act of 1925, which guaranteed farmers a price for beets. The subsidy was to have been removed by October 1934; following an enquiry by the Greene Committee in 1934, the British Sugar Corporation was set up in 1936 and took over all factories. Shareholders received compensation in shares and cash. The Bury group had proved very profitable for Tate and Lyle and so too did the terms of compensation. In 1987 Tate and Lyle tried to take over the factory again; they bid for BSC in competition with the Italian firm Gruppo Ferruzzi. Both were blocked, but by 1990 Beresford International had acquired BSC and, in that year, sold to Associated British Foods.

Records at SRO (B)
These are very limited and consist almost entirely of press cuttings.
K 768/1 Album of photographs illustrating construction of the sugar beet factory (1925). File of Newspaper cuttings of Hollow Road Beet Sugar Factory (filed under Hollow Road in Parish box files): cuttings from 1925 to 1990; photograph of German diffusers being imported 1954.

See also: P. Chalmin, *The Making of a Sugar Giant: Tate and Lyle 1859-1989* (1990).

British Sugar, Ipswich
Sugar processing

This was one of the rash of beet processing factories to be built after the First World War, and marked the beginnings of what was to become a major industry in the region. It was encouraged by the 1925 Sugar Industry (subsidy) Act. The factory was built 1924-5 by the Anglo-Dutch Sugar Company on 100 acre site at Sproughton, chosen because of good railway links. The original capacity was for 1,200 tons of beet per day and the factory also refined sugar. The Anglo-Dutch group was the largest of five groups which built factories in the 1920s; the company also had factories in Cantley, Kelham (Nottingham), Ely and King's Lynn. Initially the management was Dutch as was much of the equipment. In 1936 the British Sugar Corporation was formed and this and other factories were absorbed.

Records deposited at SRO (I) HC 429:
[The records are annotated in the class list - not catalogued in detail]
Wages book 1932-5; campaign book 1928-1968; refining book 1939;
History of the works, 1924-1988 by J. Langford - (this is very skimpy being a typescript of technical changes in works, with site plan).

Burton, Son & Sanders, Ipswich
Confectionery supplies

The firm was established 1824 by Charles Burton and expanded under subsequent generations to supply all commodities for bakers and confectioners. From the 1880s it began producing specialised products trading nationally. In 1897 Burton and Son amalgamated with Erat Sanders & Company of Colchester to form Burton, Son & Sanders as a private limited company, with branches throughout the country. In 1920 it went public. In the decades of the 1950s and 1960s the business expanded through acquisition and, in 1970, merged with Matthews Holdings and began to concentrate on exports. In 1977 Matthews Holdings was bought by Borthwick & Sons Ltd, an Ipswich company specialising in edible cake decorations. In 1993 Borthwick sold Burtons in two lots, the major part to Unilever.

Records deposited at SRO (I) HC 449:
History of the Company - miscellaneous items including a history '150 years of progress, 1824-1974' with later additions; Items for history 1883-1887 - commodity sales, employee memoirs; photographs; press cuttings from 1951; subsidiary companies from 1938; Eastern area sales; plans and buildings; photos; Matthews, from 1972; visitors book; royal warrants etc.; 1980s review; acquisitions from 1987; product brochures, from 1970; product costings and profitability 1957-80; closure of company 1990-3.

Cooperative Wholesale Society Canning Factory, Lowestoft
Food preserving

The Cooperative Wholesale Society opened a factory in Great Yarmouth, Norfolk, in 1918. In 1929, when the premises there had become outgrown, the factory was moved to Waveney Drive, Lowestoft, to a site previously owned by the Maconochie Brothers and known as 'Maconochie's Number 1'. At this time the factory was mainly concerned with canning fish, but by the 1950s was also handling meat and vegetables. In the 1970s the plant was considered outdated and an industrial dispute in 1979 almost led to its closure. However, by 1982 the factory was again profitable and in the late 1980s £15 million was spent on modernising it. An increasing proportion of its sales were to non-Co-op firms. In May 1994 the factory (known as F.E. Barber) was sold to Hobson, and in October canning work ceased with the loss of 350 jobs. The factory continued to produce 'own-brand' foods for a number of supermarket chains but was finally closed in 1997.

Records deposited at SRO (L) Ac no 1189:
Correspondence 1929-49; wages account books 1932-56; wage summary books 1936-46; employment forms and medical reports 1930-40 (access currently closed); plans 1931-40 (17); poster c1940; Great Yarmouth Fish Depot: wages summary 1926-27.

Cranfield Brothers Ltd, College Street, Ipswich
Milling and baking

The business was founded in 1884 by John George Cranfield (1860-1908). A farmer's son from Buckden, Huntingdonshire, he was first apprenticed to a local miller, Bowyer & Priestly, before gaining experience in a large flour mill at Minneapolis, USA. He subsequently converted an old stone mill in Northern Ireland to the new technique of steel roller milling and then in 1884 set up in partnership with his brother Thomas and erected the Dock Roller Mills beside the quay at Ipswich. Milling machinery made by the Ipswich engineers, E.R. & F. Turner, capable of producing eight sacks (one ton) of flour an hour was installed. The business expanded rapidly; it imported wheat from North America and built up its own fleet of lighters to unload the grain and transport it to the mill. In 1906 further land was acquired and developed to accommodate more advanced milling plant and machinery.

Cranfield's mill at Ipswich quay. Established in 1884, the mill expanded rapidly, many of the buildings dating from around 1912.

Cranfield's delivery van, c1913

Following the death of the founder in 1908, the business was converted into a private limited company, Samuel Armstrong (a relative who had joined the company in 1893) becoming its first managing director and remaining so until his death in 1959. The company continued to expand, working at full capacity throughout the two World Wars. William Green & Sons Ltd of Brantham and another Ipswich company, A.A. Gibbons Ltd, were acquired in 1953 and 1960 respectively; the mills were subsequently sold and the flour trade absorbed. During the 1930s, modern automated plant bakeries began to replace the many small craftsmen-bakers, a trend that accelerated after 1945. The company had acquired a Kent bakery company in 1936, but for a decade from the late 1950s invested heavily in building up its bakery interests. A subsidiary company, Betabake (Anglia) Ltd was formed in 1963, and a new bakery was opened at Norwich in 1966; by 1969 the company had bakeries at Ipswich, Chelmsford, Romford, Gillingham, Hayes (Middlesex) and Luton. In 1969 Cranfields began the process of modernising its milling plant (much of it unchanged since 1906); new plant was opened in March 1970 with further extensions in June (with a capacity of seventy sacks – almost nine tons – an hour) and the following January. The modernisation programme was completed in October 1970 with the opening of new offices, laboratory and test bakery at College Street. By 1971 Cranfields, the largest privately-owned independent milling-bakery group in the country, employed a workforce of 2,450 and operated a fleet of approximately 950 vehicles.

In May 1972 Cranfields was acquired by Associated British Foods Limited. The mill was put under the umbrella of Allied Mills and the Betabake bakeries became part of Allied Bakeries. In 1973 the Vitbe manufacturing plant was moved from Crayford mill to Cranfields. An on-going programme of modernisation included new packing plant, mixing facilities and bulk outloading silo. However, the continuing need for heavy capital investment together with the limitations and location of the site, led to the decision in the 1990s to close Cranfields and concentrate further investment in the north-west of the country. In October 1998 the first departments were closed with the remainder following in December 1999.

Records deposited at SRO (I) HC 464:
Probate and will of J.G. Cranfield (1908) and papers 1907-16; Memoranda and articles of association 1908; register of members and share ledger, 1908-47; directors' minutes 1908-56; private cash book/journal 1948-72; ledgers: nominal 1908-78 (includes balance sheet 1963-78); dividends 1909-63; private 1910-39 (includes profit and loss accounts and balance sheets); 1948-c71; debenture interest 1927-34; interest (bakers) 1942-71; capital

expenditure 1948-74; balance sheets and profit and loss accounts 1908-17; financial statements and reports 1922-71; pension fund records 1933-78; group bakery accounts 1964-1970s; stock valuations 1939-77; registers of English and foreign wheat 1964-98; register of vessels, freight and cargoes 1962-81; staff hours and wages records 1909-79; accident books 1964-81; schedule of securities and properties etc, 1895-1970; papers and correspondence re articles of association, depression in flour-milling trade, agreements etc 1924-38; miscellaneous newspaper articles/cuttings; photographs c1900 to 80s; printed histories, recipes and promotional material 1925-80s; E.R. & F.Turner, inventory 1918.

Records of subsidiary companies:

William Green & Sons Ltd, Brantham: Share certificates book 1912-55; financial statements and reports 1935-67; agreement and declaration of trust 1938; ledgers 1942-58.

AA. Gibbons Ltd: Share certificates book 1922-60; private ledgers 1931-54.

Jasper & Son: Minutes 1904-56; annual returns 1954-58.

Banks Bakeries Ltd, Harrietsham, Kent: Ledger 1960-66.

John Crisp & Son Ltd, Beccles
Malting

The business was founded by John Crisp (1707-1778), merchant and maltster, of Wangford, Suffolk, and continued by seven successive generations of John Crisp. John II (1752-1802), like his father a merchant and maltster, moved to Beccles towards the end of the eighteenth century where he established one of the best known East Anglian malting businesses. He built large maltings at Beccles and purchased his cousin William's maltings at Southwold when he died in 1844. By the mid-nineteenth century the firm was making malt on commission for the big London brewers, Meux and Calverts, and became one of the main commission agents for the Burton brewer, Allsopps. The business was registered as a private limited company in 1909 with a capital of £40,000. It was acquired by the Leeds maltster, W.J. Robson & Company in 1927 and the following year, Robsons and Crisps became two of the five founding companies of Associated British Maltsters Ltd.

Records deposited at SRO (I) HC461 (as part of the Pauls Malt Archive):
Board Minutes 1956; ledger 1949-58; plans 1932-51; fire insurance specification 1958-59;

deeds c1700-c1930; abstract of title to maltings and premises in Thetford, Norfolk (Bullard & Sons Ltd) 1924-27.

See also: Rachel Lawrence, *Southwold River: Georgian Life in the Blyth Valley* (1990) pp.78-83.

G & J Cutting, Pettaugh
Milling

George and James Cutting are first listed in Kelly's 1883 directory as farmers and millers. They are shown as roller millers, corn and flour merchants by the First World War. The business, registered as a private limited company by the 1930s, was acquired by the Yorkshire company, A-One Feed Supplements Ltd, in June 1997.

Records deposited at SRO (I): HC 454
Minute book 1950-53; ledgers 1912-50; day book 1929-30; annual accounts 1916-36; cash book 1932-40; Mr G.W. French's commission 1938-48; production book 1950-53; market book 1950-53; grain receipt book 1955-6; threshing records 1943-45; diaries 1952, 1962, 1965; plan of extension to mill (nd).
Records from the period of Government control, 1939-50:
10th and 11th control year records, including sales day books, wages books, Ministry of Food returns, grain receipt books, purchase book for home grown wheat and American wheat, weekly production sheets of flour, offals and self-raising flour, weekly stock sheets.

Greene, King & Sons Plc, Bury St Edmunds
Brewing

The business was founded c1806 by Benjamin Greene when he formed a partnership with William Buck and opened the Westgate Brewery at Bury St Edmunds. By 1833 the firm supplied free trade beer as far afield as Newmarket. Edward Greene, Benjamin's third son, took over the management of the brewery after his father's death in 1836. The business expanded rapidly during the 1840s and 1850s and had acquired public houses by the end of the 1860s. Another Bury St Edmunds brewer, Henry Braddock, was acquired in 1868 and Philips Brothers of Stowmarket in 1882. Greene King & Sons Ltd was registered as a limited liability company in June 1887 to acquire and merge the businesses of E. Greene & Son and F.W. King & Son (established 1868), of St Edmund's Brewery, Westgate Street, Bury St Edmunds. The new company continued to take over other brewers: Thomas Jenner, Haverhill, Suffolk, in 1887; Jabez Rankin, Braintree, Essex, and Thomas Charlton, Fakenham, Norfolk, in 1891; Charles F. Moody, Newmarket, Suffolk, in 1896; Snell & Raven, Wethersfield, Essex, in 1902; Oliver Gosling, Bocking, Essex, in 1904; Clarke Bros, Bury St Edmunds, in 1917; F.C. Christmas & Company, Haverhill, in 1918; Oliver Bros. Sudbury, Suffolk, in 1919; Bailey & Tebbutt, Cambridge, in 1925; Ogden & Sons, March, Cambridgeshire, in 1930; Rayment & Company Ltd, Furneaux Pelham, Hertfordshire(closed 1987), in 1931; Thomas Prentice & Company, Stowmarket, Suffolk, in 1934; E. Gardner & Son, Little Coggeshall, Essex, in 1943; Simpson's Brewery Ltd, Baldock, Hertfordshire, in 1954 (renamed Greene King (Baldock) Ltd), in 1963; Herbert Cawdron & Son Ltd, wine merchants, in 1954; J.C. Mauldon & Sons, Sudbury, in 1958; Wells & Winch Ltd, Biggleswade, Bedfordshire, in 1961 (renamed Greene King (Biggleswade) Ltd, in 1963). Greene King became one of the largest independent brewers and pub owners in the UK, with two breweries at Bury St Edmunds and Biggleswade. In 1995 the company acquired the Magic Pub Company which extended its territory across southern England. The take-over of the family-run Beards of Sussex three years later added a further forty-three properties to its estate. In 1999 the company purchased 165 pubs previously owned by Marston, Thompson & Evershed and then in July took-over Morlands of Oxfordshire who had itself acquired Ruddles.

Records held by the company at Bury St Edmunds:
Directors' minutes 1887-date; managers' meeting minutes 1919-63; public houses 1929-57; travellers and outside representatives 1936-60; general meeting papers 1940, 1953-4; share correspondence 1948-52; share transfer registers 1935-66; debenture stock: deed and agreements 1887-1982, certificate 1890-1901, ledgers 1887-1929, interest payments 1903-29, mortgage register 1887; memoranda and articles of association 1887-1954; annual returns 1959-60; seal register 1950-79; Rayment & Company purchase agreement 1923; annual reports and accounts 1927-date; annual accounts 1925-date; ledgers: private 1878-date, general 1934-60, investment 1936-50; tax statements and subsidiaries accounts 1944-50; sales books 1902-52; trade books 1914-55; price list c1920; brewing; programme 1906, card 1906, books 1923-53; stock books 1888-1969; labour book 1930-34; staff pension fund: trust deed and rules 1929, meeting minutes 1929-70; brewery proportions 1950; plant valuations 1950; public house: valuations 1950, leases 1868-1930; insurance policies and details 1964-65; press cuttings 1880-1950.

Records of Greene King (Biggleswade) Ltd are held at Church Street, Biggleswade, and at Lloyds Bank plc, 71 Lombard Street, London EC3P 3BS. For a full list see Richmond and Turton, p.160.

See also: R.G. Wilson, *Greene King: A Business and Family History* (1983)

Ind Coope Ltd, Halesworth
Brewing

The Halesworth Brewery was acquired by the Colchester Brewery Company Ltd in 1888. It was purchased by Ind Coope & Company Ltd, London, in 1925.

Records deposited at SRO (I) HC29:
[These are in a class list and not in the catalogue]
Title deed of Halesworth Brewery 1867-1910.

Ipswich Malting Company Ltd, New Cut, Ipswich
Malting

The business originated as the Flint Wharf Corn & Malting Company. On 1 July 1896 Percy Crossman paid Eugene Wells, of the Vale, Buxhall, Stowmarket, £12,500 for a half share in the business, which was renamed the Ipswich Malting Company. Two new five-floor 250 quarter maltings (Nos. 3 and 4) were built at the New Cut but were badly damaged by fire, to the cost of £50,000, in February 1900. The maltings were rebuilt but were again gutted by fire in May 1908. The following year the business was registered as a private limited company with a capital of £100,000. Further maltings were acquired at Melton Hill, Woodbridge (c1908) and, after the First World War, at Felixstowe Docks. The assets of the Newark firm of J.W. & H. Branston (which for many years had made a substantial quantity of malt for the company on commission) were acquired in 1954. Four years later, the business was purchased by H.A. & D. Taylor of Sawbridgeworth. The combined group joined Associated British Maltsters the following year.

Records deposited at SRO (I) HC461 (as part of the Pauls Malt archive):
Directors' Minutes, No 3, 1949-58; ledgers, 1895-32; Percy Crossman ledger, 1896-1906; private ledger, 1943-49; journal, 1933-67; private ledger J.W. & H. Branston, 1946-63;

accounts, 1908-28; Grain Dryers (Melton) Ltd, Journal, 1950-63; Grain Dryers (Melton) Ltd, ledger, 1950-59

Lavenham Sugar Factory
Sugar processing

Commercial extraction of sugar from beet began, in this country, only after the First World War but there were several earlier experiments. A well-known venture in Suffolk, though an ultimate commercial failure, was the sugar factory in Lavenham built by Duncan, the London refiner, in 1868. The factory was intended to extract juice for refining in Duncan's refinery in London. It always had over capacity for the local supply of beet, was never able to operate at a profit and was sold to Bolton and Partners of Westminster in 1884 and later to Roper and Sons Ltd who sold the machinery and used the building for storage from 1891.

Records in SRO (B):
HD 941: Letters proposing reopening Lavenham Sugar Works, Bolton and Partners, 27/10/1884.
HD 1319: Letters of Agreement from Bolton and Partners to J.H. Turner, Ickworth Park, to grow sugar beets; responses from J.H. Turner.
K/PF Copies of photograph of factory showing effects of fire, 1905.

See also
Sugar Beet. Some Facts and Some Illusions, by 'Home Counties' (1911)
The Sugar Beet Industry (HMSO, 1931)

B.F. Marriage, Pakenham
Milling

This is a long established business. It is unfortunate that the records cover such a limited time (1934-74) and give little indication of the history of the firm.

Records deposited at SRO (B) HC 503
These refer to the period 1934-1974. Sales Ledgers, day books, cash books, purchase ledgers, notebooks, production records, 1945-52; wages books 1959-68; desk diaries

(with memos of orders), calendars.

Charles Marston & Sons, Bungay Mill
Flour milling

Bungay water mill was acquired by Charles Marston of Brooke, Norfolk, c1875. He subsequently expanded the business of flour milling, corn and hop merchant, and seed crushing, and by 1896 had converted the mill to a roller mill. In 1900 Marston purchased Earsham Mill from Thomas Clarke; built c1863, a roller plant had been installed in 1893. The mill was remodelled by Marston in 1904 and by the 1920s had a capacity of 3½ sacks per hour. A mill was also acquired at Harleston. The firm began making self raising flour during this period. Earsham Mills were sold to Hovis Ltd in 1939 and closed in 1962.

Records deposited at SRO (L) Ac no 623:
Ledgers 1884-1915 (4 vols); day books 1902-1916 (23 vols); cash books 1898-1915 (11 vols); misc customer account books 1901-12 (3 vols); bills 1872-1907 (mainly for repairs to mill); letters 1893-1907; photograph of millers house, Bungay, nd.

See also: ac no ES 631 for records of the Marston family

J.C. Mauldon & Sons, White Horse Brewery, Sudbury
Brewing

The business was founded c1793 as a home-brewery inn. In 1868 Mrs Anna Maria Mauldon was operating the White Horse Inn, which was purchased by her son, Christie Edwin Mauldon, in 1875. They built a small brewery behind the inn to supply their nine licensed houses and acquired the business of Stephen Spurgin between 1885 and 1888. A fire destroyed the original brewery in 1900 and a larger one was rebuilt on the site. Mauldon took two of his sons, Christie and John, into partnership in 1907; they continued to run the business after his death in 1913. After the death of Christie Mauldon in 1945, John continued in partnership with his son, John. The business was acquired by Greene King & Sons Ltd, Bury St Edmunds, in 1958. At that time the firm brewed 2,000 barrels per year and owned 22 licensed premises.

Records held by Greene King & Sons plc, Westgate Brewery, Bury St Edmunds:

Profit and loss accounts 1939-57; rent ledger 1938-57; public house deeds nd.

See also: Richmond and Turton, p.230.

E. & G. Morse, Lowestoft
Brewing

Frank Morse founded the Bell Lane Brewery in 1842. By 1864 Henry Glasspool Woods, wine merchant, had joined the partnership, which traded as Morse & Woods. The firm had moved to the Crown Street Brewery by 1868 and also operated the Swaffham Brewery, White Hart Lane, Swaffham, until 1895. The firm also owned maltings at Lowestoft, Swaffham and, by the late 1870s, at Princes Street and Crown Street, Ipswich. In 1895 Henry Woods left the partnership which was restyled E. & G. Morse. The firm was acquired by Morgan's Brewery Company Ltd, Norwich, in 1936 and ceased to brew.

Records held at Adnams & Company, Sole Bay Brewery, Southwold:
Brewing books 1944-90.

Norfolk Record Office, Norwich BR 158:
Title deeds, Lowestoft, Swaffham and public houses in west and central Norfolk 1711-1919.

See also: Richmond and Turton, p.242.

C. & E. Morton Ltd, Lowestoft
Canning and preserving

J.T. Morton opened a small canning factory in Aberdeen in 1847 for supplying tinned food to sailing ships. He later expanded the business to London where the company had factories in Leadenhall Street, Millwall and Poplar. On his death in 1897 his two sons, Charles and Edward, took over, the company being renamed C. & E. Morton Ltd. In 1900 a site was acquired in Lowestoft for a fish processing plant. Other factories were set up at Mevagissey, Cornwall, and Bristol, the headquarters remaining at The Minories, London. By 1902 The Lowestoft factory had become the largest herring canning factory in Britain; it concentrated on canning for export, with products sent all over the world.

It was a major supplier to the British army serving in India and elsewhere, and also supplied many expeditions such as the Shackleton and Scott Polar expeditions. During the Great War canned beef and vegetables were sent to the troops in France. Several countries began canning their own produce during the war, and in the inter-war period other products were introduced to compensate – fish and meat pastes and soups - and from 1938 Morton's products were introduced onto the home market. In the Second World War the company made ration packs for the forces and packed Red Cross parcels. Until the 1940s, all the tins used were made on site; subsequently the contract was given to Metal Box Ltd. In 1945 Beechams gained a controlling interest although the company continued to trade under its own name. Vegetable canning – processed, mushy and garden peas, broad and runner beans – became the main products, with the Field Department contracting local farmers to grow and harvest vegetables. Fruit fillings were introduced in the 1960s, together with several confectionery lines – peppermints, Murraymints and Mac throat sweets. In the quiet season pickles, soups, pastes, gravy salt and baked beans were produced. Mortons also began to process foods for many of the large supermarket chains as well as own label. On 8 December 1986 the business was sold to Hillsdown Holdings for £8.5m. In April 1988 the factory was closed. The site was purchased by a development group in 1991 and the factory subsequently demolished.

Records deposited at SRO (L) Ac no 963:
Kitchen Office daily production output book, 1940-86; sample register - details and description of product, recipe etc 1941-46; retort cooking and cooling schedules, 1952-55; files of specification for products, raw materials, production methods, packaging etc, 1948-86; buying priorities, rules and procedures, 1953; products estimates books, 1901-29; estimates sheets (as above), 1915-28; tin estimates, 1910-29; loose tin estsimates nd, c1910-29; correspondence, 1915-16 (two letters); cuttings of Mortons weekly export list prices for herrings, 1903-13.

See also: A.R. Charlesworth, *The Morton Story: The Lowestoft Food Factory, 1901-1988* (privately published, 1995)

Muntons plc, Stowmarket
Malting and malt products

The business was founded by Munton Baker-Munton in 1921. His father, Horace (a partner in the London malt and barley factors, Munton & Baker), had already established a small business importing malt extract from the United States. As demand for the product increased after the First World War, Baker-Munton decided to establish a British-based manufacturing plant to supply malt extract to brewers, the bakery and tonic food industries. Operating from the old Phoenix brewery owned by the Bedford Brewers, Charles Wells Limited (who became major shareholders), the business, initially known as Munton & Baker (Bedford) Limited, was renamed Muntona in 1923. Besides malt extract, the company introduced a range of malt products: 'Muntona Malted Soap', 'Maltona' cattle and horse feed, 'Yeaso' high protein yeast food and 'Renu-glo' starch solvent for laundries.

In 1935 the Ipswich firm of Edward Fison was acquired. An old-established maltster, in 1903 Fisons had been one of the first British companies to diversify into the production of malt extract for brewers and bakers. The rationalisation of the two firms was delayed by the war but in November 1947 a derelict industrial site at Stowmarket, previously owned by British Nylon Spinners, was purchased. A new malt extract plant and mechanised maltings were opened in 1950 (and further extended in 1959 and 1962). Three years later the Ipswich extract factory and maltings were closed followed, in 1959, by the Bedford plant. In 1958 the company changed its name to Munton & Fison Ltd.

During this period the company fostered a growing interest in export markets (especially to Germany and the British Commonwealth); by 1962 exports to twenty-nine countries accounted for 10 per cent of production. Sales to the Scotch whisky distilling industry also became increasingly important and in 1963 Munton & Fison, in a joint enterprise with two distilling companies, Invergordon and Highland Distillers, built the Flamborough Maltings at Bridlington, in Yorkshire. Five years later, the venture, which had revived the name of Edward Fison Ltd, became a wholly owned subsidiary of Munton & Fison. Expansion at Stowmarket continued: a new malt extract plant was commissioned in 1971 and, seven years later, the Cedar Maltings. The firm also diversified, entering the home brew market (with Tom Caxton and Brewmaker kits) in 1977 then, to utilise surplus low-grade heat from malting, moving into fish farming, hydroponics and plant micropropagation. A series of acquisitions followed: in 1988, the malt flour business of Associated British Maltsters; three years later the Bildeston corn merchants, C.K. Squirrell & Sons (q.v.) and D. Quinton & Sons (also located on the Stowmarket site), manufacturers of pet foods; in 1992, the grain drying and storage facilities of R.M. English & Son Ltd at Full Sutton, Yorkshire, and, in 1997, the seedsmen, Simpsons Bros (Darsham) Ltd and the Scottish maltster, Robert Kilgour. The company was renamed Muntons plc in 1996.

Records held by the company (enquiries to: the Company Secretary, Muntons plc, Cedars Maltings, Stowmarket, Suffolk, IP14 2AG):

Articles of association, Munton & Baker (Bedford) Ltd, Muntona Ltd, Edward Fison Ltd and Munton & Fison Ltd; share certificate books, Muntona (16 vols), Munton & Fison (2 vols); settlement between War Department and Muntona re old silk mills 1956.

Munton & Fison: directors' minutes, 1955-94; annual returns to Companies House, to 1978; share transfers and correspondence 1971-79; Cedars Factory deeds and documents.

Edward Fison Ltd: annual returns; original share register; miscellaneous documents.

D. Quinton & Sons: directors' minutes, 1940-91; share transfer document; share registers (2 vols); pension scheme (2 vols).

The company's records are to be deposited at SRO (I)

See also: Jonathan Mardle, 'A Growing Business: The Story of Muntons Plc' (typescript).

Pauls Malt Ltd, Kentford, Newmarket
Malting

The staff of R.& W. Paul at the Boltons, the home of Robert Stocker Paul, for their annual garden party, c1908

The business was founded by Robert Paul (who had previously managed the small family brewery in Foundation Street, Ipswich and its tied estate of fifteen public houses and a wine and spirit trade) c1842. On his death in 1864 it comprised eleven small maltings and six barges. After a decade of administration by executors the business passed to his sons, Robert Stocker (1845-1909) and William Francis (1850-1928) and thereafter expanded rapidly. In 1893 it was incorporated as a private limited company, R. & W. Paul Ltd, with a share capital of £250,000. New maltings and a factory for dressing foreign barley had been built at Ipswich and maltings rented at Woodbridge, Stowmarket and Stonham. The company had also diversified into the manufacture of animal feedstuffs and flaked maize for brewers and built up an impressive shipping fleet. Maize and barley were imported from America and eastern Europe, and malt, barley and smaller quantities of wheat and oats were shipped outwards, accounting for some two-thirds of the grain exported from Ipswich. In 1902 Pauls purchased Gillman & Spencer Ltd of Rotherhithe (manufacturers of flaked maize and brewers' preservatives), where they developed Kositos, an animal feed made from cooked flaked maize, for which the company was known for many decades. In 1904, the first of two 300 quarter maltings was built at the New Cut at Stoke, Ipswich; the second was completed in 1912, the complex remaining the centrepiece of the enterprise for several decades. In 1906 a financial interest was taken in the Grantham malting company, Lee & Grinling Limited and in 1914 the Barnetby (Lincolnshire) maltings of Truswell's Brewery Company were purchased. Boal Mill at Kings Lynn was purchased in 1912 and converted for the production of animal foodstuffs. In 1918 the Hull Malt Company, manufacturers of flaked maize, was acquired and converted for milling animal feeds. Expansion continued throughout the inter-war years with full control of Lee & Grinling achieved in 1928. The Albion Sugar Company, producing invert sugars for the brewing trade, was registered in 1929 (a joint venture with White Tomkins & Courage). The Leeds firm of Richard Dobson & Son was purchased in 1941 and, three years later, the Thetford maltings of James Fison Limited. However, the main emphasis during the period was on the company's animal feed interests especially the new growth area of compound feeds. New mills were built at the Manchester Ship Canal (1931), Avonmouth Docks (1934) and Faversham (1935), and those at Ipswich, Kings Lynn, Hull and London were extended and re-equipped.

To facilitate a major investment programme, the company went public in 1960 and three years later merged with White Tomkins & Courage. A new holding company, Pauls & Whites, was formed, with five wholly-owned subsidiaries - Gillman & Spencer, the Albion Sugar Company, White Tomkins & Courage, Pauls Foods and R.& W. Paul

(Maltsters) - the last two formed by separating Pauls' milling and malting interests. Modern maltings were built at Ipswich, Grantham and Mendlesham, but expansion of the malting division was mainly by acquisition: in 1965 S. Swonnell & Sons of Oulton Broad [q.v.] and Harrington Page of Ware; in 1969 Sandars & Company of Gainsborough (and its subsidiaries, J. Pidcock & Company Ltd of Nottingham and Yeomans, Cherry & Curtis of Burton-upon-Trent); three years later the Scottish maltster, Robert Hutchison & Company. European subsidiaries followed: in 1971 a quarter share in the Belgian company, Malteries Huys NV; in 1973, the French companies, Usines Ethel SA and its neighbour, Grands Moulins de Strasbourg, and in 1977, a German subsidiary, Malzfabrik Schragmalz. In 1985 Pauls was acquired by the overseas trading and plantations group, Harrisons & Crosfield. Two years later Pauls purchased Associated British Maltsters (formed in 1928 from the merger of five leading malting firms), becoming the largest European malting company. The economic downturn of the early 1990s brought the closure of maltings at Grimsby and Kirkcaldy in 1992 and two years later at Ware. Pauls purchased the Glenesk Maltings, near Montrose, from United Distillers in January 1997 and in February 1998 commissioned a new malting at Bury St Edmunds; its annual capacity of 100,000 tonnes making the site the largest in Europe. Two months later, following the decision by H.& C. to focus on their core business of chemicals, Pauls Malt was sold to the Irish-based agriculture and sugar conglomerate, Greencore.

The Pauls Malt archive represents the major collection relating to the British malting industry. It includes records of many subsidiary companies, notably Associated British Maltsters. Although several of these are fragmented, together they provide an unparalleled record of the industry.

Records deposited at SRO (I) HC461:
Pauls Malt: directors' minutes, Nov 1893-Apr 1941; general meetings minute book, 1894-1954; agreement between Elizabeth Paul and R.S. Paul 1870; conveyance between R.S. Paul and W.F. Paul, 1871; R.& W. Paul balance sheets, 1894-1967; Pauls malt annual report and accounts 1961-86; registers: stock and shares 1918-65, members and share ledger 1959-76, directors' holdings and interests 1948-57, ordinary shareholders' accounts c1920-c60; private journals 1893-1966; ledgers: 1881-86, private 1886-1969, capital 1902-07, personal 1901-60, revenue 1901-25, property; salaries ledger 1899-1926; clerks' salaries 1927-48; wages 1932-64; King's Lynn 1932-34; wages book (including POWs at Stonham Maltings) 1940; conditions of employment; foreign barley purchases 1920-40; sales/deliveries 1894-65; ABM/Pauls reports re specific projects 1969-83; superannuation fund: minutes 1908-40, members' ledgers 1908-65, journals 1934-c65;

contributory pension fund journals 1939-67; pension scheme 1964-69; housing trust: journal 1917-42, ledger 1917-42, cash books 1917-30; Pauls Benevolent Fund minutes 1957-62; shipping records: private journal 1902-07, private ledger 1902-49, barge and motor vessel arrivals 1962-64, cargoes grain resale 1903-22; Broxtead Estate: farm acounts 1921-43, 1965-78, rates 1930-44, rents 1934-52, 55-72, ledger 1955-79, annual stocktaking 1968-78; deeds for various properties including Union Jack, the Quay, Ipswich 1770-1876, St Peter's Mills, Ipswich 1731-1866, Smarts Wharf, Ipswich; Newsletters 1960-97; photographs and newscuttings 20th century.

Records of subsidiary companies:
Lee & Grinling, Grantham; Gillman & Spencer Limited, Rotherhithe; Sandars & Company Limited, Gainsborough; J. Pidcock & Company Limited, Nottingham; Yeomans, Cherry & Curtis, Burton-upon-Trent; Henry Page & Company Limited, Ware.

Associated British Maltsters – ABM (formed in July 1928 from five old-established family firms: Gilstrap Earp Limited, Newark-upon-Trent; Edward Sutcliffe Limited, Mirfield; Samuel Thompson & Sons, Smethwick; W.J. Robson & Company, Leeds, and their subsidiary (acquired in 1927), John Crisp & Son, Beccles).
The deposit includes ABM Directors' Minutes, 1928-1968; some records of: Gilstrap Earp; William Glossop & Bulay Ltd, Hull; Reynold, Stott & Haslegrove Ltd, Wakefield; W.J.Robson & Company Ltd, Leeds; Michael Sanderson & Son Ltd, Wakefield; H.A.& D. Taylor Ltd, Sawbridgeworth; Richard Worsick & Son Ltd, Wakefield.

See also: Christine Clark, *The British Malting Industry Since 1830* (Hambledon Press, 1998)
Roger Finch, *A Cross in the Topsail: An account of the shipping interests of R.& W. Paul Ltd, Ipswich* (Boydell Press, Ipswich, 1979)
B.A. Holderness, 'Pauls of Ipswich: History of the Family and of the Company of R.& W. Paul Ltd to 1963 and of Pauls & Whites Ltd from 1963 to 1978' (Typescript, 1980)
E.F. Taylor, 'History of the formation and development of Associated British Maltsters Ltd 1926-1978' (Typescript, 1978)
'The Hutchisons of Kirkcaldy: A History of the Family and Firm' (Typescript, nd.)
All at SRO (I).

Key Street, Ipswich, the head office of R.& W. Paul, in 1912

Pauls' cricket team, 1906, typical of those run by many companies.

J.E. Pettit & Sons, Redgrave Mill
Milling

Records deposited at SRO (I) HC416:

Ledgers 1931-37 (3 vols); purchase cash books 1943-70 (4 vols); sales day books – mill 1958-64 (2 vols); sales day books – poultry and eggs 1953-65 (4 vols); wages book 1939-50; analysis of expenditure book 1944-65; stock record including notes of investments 1949-54; analyses and calculations – animal feeding stuffs; Redgrave Tower Windmill, copy deeds 1740-1903 (34 items).

C. K. Squirrell & Sons Ltd, Bildeston
Malting and corn merchanting

William Squirrell (b1781), a clock and barometer manufacturer, began the family business at Bildeston. His son, William II, diversified into farming and trading in wines, and became an agent for the Norwich Union Insurance Company (a role which continued until the mid 1990s). In 1872, maltings were built at 125, High Street, Bildeston. By the end of the First World War the business had concentrated on corn merchanting. A family firm through seven generations, the business was registered as a private limited company in 1954. It was acquired by Muntons in 1992. The Bildeston site was vacated in 1995 and the business re-located on the Muntons site at Stowmarket.

Records held by Muntons plc (enquiries to: the Company Secretary, Muntons plc, Cedars Maltings, Stowmarket, Suffolk, IP14 2AG):

Directors' minutes 1954-90; Debenture and certificate of registration 1991.

Records privately held:

William Squirrell's diary 1840-80; Norwich Union insurance premium records 1830 to early 1900s.

Patrick Stead, Halesworth
Malting

Patrick Stead (after training with a London grain merchant) set up as a corn merchant and factor at Great Yarmouth, Norfolk, c1815. He initially had two Scottish partners (Thomas MacKenzie and John Robinson) but after 1832 continued as sole proprietor. From the 1820s the firm rented maltings throughout Norfolk and Suffolk, dispatched malt and barley to London, Liverpool and Hull, and made substantial quantities of malt for the big London brewers, Truman, Hanbury & Buxton. By the 1840s the business was thought to be the largest malting concern in the country. Thirty-six maltsters were employed in 1851.

In 1838 Stead moved his headquarters to Halesworth, Suffolk, where he built a large complex of seven new maltings, including a revolutionary malting system which he patented in 1842. This used steam and hot air to control germination and kilning. In 1849, shortly before his retirement to his native Scotland, Stead sold the entire business to Trumans who continued to operate the maltings throughout the following century.

Records deposited at Norfolk Record Office:
Articles of partnership, 1817

Records deposited at Greater London Record Office B/THB (as part of the Truman Hanbury & Buxton archive):
Truman Hanbury & Buxton, barley ledgers; Thursday private minutes; River Blythe navigation shares.

See also: R. Lawrence, 'An Early Nineteenth Century Malting Business in East Suffolk', *Proceedings of the Suffolk Institute of Archaeology*, XXXVI (2), 1986, pp.115-129.

S. Swonnell & Son Ltd, Snape and Oulton Broad
Malting

Swonnells, originally based at Nine Elms, Battersea, was one of the oldest established malting companies and, by the early nineteenth century, one of the leading London malt factors. As the role of the factors gradually declined the business specialised in the production of roasted and coloured malts. It was incorporated as a limited company in 1898 with a capital of £50,000 and merged with another old-established maltster and malt roasting company, Tomkins, Courage & Cracknell, also of London. Two years later the business moved to Oulton Broad in Suffolk where new maltings were built to gain the dual advantage of good barley land and access to coastal and rail transport. In

October 1918 the Snape maltsters, Newson Garrett & Son Ltd (founded in 1841 by Newson Garrett, younger son of the well-known agricultural engineer, Richard Garrett [q.v.]), was acquired for £40,500. Also specialists in roasted and coloured malts, the two firms had been associated for many years. Another small company with whom there were long links, Alfred Gough Ltd of Saffron Walden, was purchased in 1955; the Saffron Walden maltings were closed and the business transferred to Snape. Ten years later, the London company, Randells (Maltsters) Ltd, was also acquired. Later in 1965 Swonnells was bought by Pauls of Ipswich for £75,000. The Snape maltings were sold and subsequently developed as the famous concert hall. The Oulton Broad maltings were modernised in 1966 but were closed two years later during a sharp recession in the malting trade; they have subsequently been redeveloped for housing.

Records deposited at SRO (I) HC461 (as part of the Pauls Malt archive):
Articles of Association 1898; private ledgers, 1898-1954 (6 vols); ledger, malt trading account 1900-32; private journal 1914-65; journal 1965-66; manufacturing costs and balance sheets, 1910-37; list of employees 1901-68; Works Committee minutes 1963-65.

Records deposited at SRO (L) Ac no 314:
Conveyance of land in Oulton 1846; plans 1900-02, relating mainly to building of new maltings; patents and specifications 1912-16 (16); Oulton tithe rent charge 1914-37; rights of way, extract from deeds etc, 1912-23.

See also: Robert Simper, 'The Story of Snape Maltings', *East Anglian Magazine*, 1967.

Tollemache & Cobbold Brewery Ltd, Cliff Brewery, Ipswich
Brewing

In 1723 Thomas Cobbold began brewing at Harwich, Essex, but moved to the Cliff Brewery, Ipswich in 1746. The business steadily built up a large tied estate of public houses and came to dominate brewing in the town. In 1923 a further twenty-eight licensed properties were acquired from Catchpole & Company, the Unicorn Brewery, Ipswich, when it ceased trading. The following March, Cobbold & Company was registered as a private limited liability company. In 1957 this company merged with another Ipswich brewer, Tollemache's Breweries Ltd to form Tollemache & Cobbold Breweries Ltd. Tollemache Brothers had been established in 1888 with the purchase of the Brooke Street Brewery (opened in 1856) from Charles Cullingham on his retirement.

Tollemache's Ipswich Brewery Ltd was registered in May 1896; it acquired Collier Brothers, Essex Brewery, Walthamstow, London, in August 1920 and was renamed Tollemache's Breweries Limited. It also acquired Barwell & Sons, Norwich (wine and spirits merchants) in 1921, the other twenty-eight public houses of Catchpole & Company in 1923, the Star Brewery (Cambridge) Limited (and 120 public houses) in 1934, and Frederick George Stone, Tollesbury Essex in 1950. Following the merger with Cobbold & Company, the Cliff Brewery was extended in 1959 and 1961 when the Brooke Street Brewery was closed; all the firm's brewing was concentrated at the Cliff Brewery in 1972. Five years later the business with its 360 public houses was acquired by the Ellerman Shipping Group (who in 1975 had purchased J.W. Cameron of Hartlepool) for £5.7 million. In 1983 Ellerman sold its brewing interests to the property developers, David and Frederick Barclay who subsequently sold them to Brent Walker. In July 1989 all production was transferred to the Lion Brewery at Hartlepool and the Cliff Brewery closed. Following a management buy-out, the business began trading again in July 1990 with the Cliff Brewery reopening in September.

Records deposited at SRO (I) HA231

Cobbold & Company:

Deeds concerning family marriage settlement and mortgage 1762-1874; partnership agreements 1857-1923; brewery mortgage 1858; declaration of value, rentals and inns 1858; profit and loss books 1866-1900; partnership account book 1894-1919; annual accounts and balance sheet 1898-1919; summary cash book 1932-46; wages book: brewery 1875-1941; bottling stores 1929-38, 1948-49; ledgers (general, private, paid, town, loan and deposit, sales and rent, 1878-1961); daily bottled beer sales 1929-44.

Tollemache & Cobbold Breweries Ltd:

Sales particulars and accounts, Cullingham Brewery 1887-88; sales ledger 1958-59.

(The records listed in L. Richmond and A. Turton (eds), *The Brewing Industry: a Guide to Historical Records* (1990), pp. 108-09, 333-34, are believed to have been destroyed).

See also: Michael Jacobson, *The Cliff Brewery 1723-1973* (Ipswich, 1973)

Robert Malster, *250 Years of Brewing in Ipswich* (Ipswich, 1996)

Watney Mann & Truman Maltings Ltd, Staithe Maltings, Bungay
Malting

The Bungay maltings were purchased in 1919 by the London brewers, Watney Combe Reid, from E. Walker as part of the Waveney Valley group of maltings with sites at Bungay, Harleston and Halesworth. Subsequently maltings at Tivetshall and Long Melford were acquired. In 1973, following the formation of Watney Mann & Truman Holdings, the maltings were known as Watney Mann & Truman Maltings Ltd; they were sold to the maltsters, J.P. Simpson (Alnwick) Ltd, of Berwick-on-Tweed, in 1986. The Bungay maltings were closed in 1984 and sold for housing re-development.

Records deposited at SRL (L) Ac nos 594 and 1253

Ledger c1920-30s (accounts for malthouse working expenses, freight, roast house working expenses, barley); wage account sheet 1926; Norwich hospitals and medical list, Sunday and Saturday Contributor's Fund, collector's book 1921-26 (five vols); Outing Club subscriptions book, 1924; plan, furnace for sweating drum plant, 1955; invoices for works outing 1922; crystal malt report c1930; extraction amounts for English crystal malt 1933.

PRINTING

The first commercial steam-powered printing press, installed by William Clowes in his London works in 1823.

Clays Ltd, Bungay

The company was founded by Richard Clay who was born in Cambridge in 1789. Having been apprenticed to the University Printer in 1803, Clay became manager of a London printer, Burton & Briggs, in 1818, acquiring the business in 1827. Two years later he moved to Bread Street Hill where he carried out a wide range of printing work; by 1839, he employed twenty-six journeyman compositors and fourteen apprentices. The firm became known for its expert printing of wood engravings and coloured gift books, often elaborately illustrated and bound, and worked for many leading publishers. In 1857, Clay went into partnership with Joseph Taylor; on Taylor's retirement in 1868, his two sons Charles and Richard formed a new partnership, R. Clay, Sons & Taylor. The young Richard was one of the most technically minded printers of the time, and in 1872 patented improvements to the 'Wharfedale' type of cylinder printer.

In 1876, Clays bought the Bungay business of Childs & Son following the death of its founder, John Childs. Established in 1798 by Richard Morris and Charles Brightly, the firm had specialised in copperplate engravings. John Childs married Brightly's daughter and took over the firm in 1823. Like the Clays, Childs was technically innovative and the two firms worked together for many years. The relatively low wages of the skilled workforce, at a time of increasing competition from Scottish and provincial printers, made the business doubly attractive. The firm was renamed the Chaucer Press. In 1911 a new, larger factory was opened at Brunswick Street, Southwark; it was sold to the periodical publishers, Iliffe & Sons Limited of Coventry and London, in 1920. A London firm of process engravers, Noakes Bros Ltd was acquired in 1938. Destroyed by bombing in 1941, the factory was rebuilt and remained a subsidiary company until 1950 when it was sold to The Amalgamated Press. Expansion at Bungay continued after 1918. Although Clays were still general printers, the inter-war years saw the gradual acceleration of the shift to a major book-printing firm. The formation of Penguin Books Ltd in 1935 not only marked a revolution in British book publishing, for Clays, who printed some of their first paperbacks, it represented a new avenue for expansion which was to grow throughout the 1940s and 1950s. Clays was registered as a public company in 1956. A two-year programme of work-study and measurement provided the foundations for restructuring into a modern group. Fletcher & Sons Ltd, of Norwich, an old-established firm of lithographic printers, was purchased in 1961. Two years later, to complement the company's expertise in the production of long-run book work (focused mainly on educational textbooks), a share in Northumberland Press Ltd, Gateshead, specialists in short-run fiction composition and printing, was acquired (printing was discontinued in 1977). During the mid 1970s Clays expanded its base by moving into export markets, mainly Scandinavia. The colour printers, Cox & Wyman, of Fakenham, were purchased in 1979 (and closed two years later, a victim of recession). The following year, a pilot plant was established in Singapore to take advantage of lower production costs and the growth potential of the market; printing and binding departments were added in 1981. Late in 1985, Clays joined the St Ives Group. The Bungay site, with a workforce of 550, is the largest owned by the group and specialises in black and white or two colour book printing. The company plans to move to a new site.

Records deposited at SRO (L) Ac no 1289:
Include: Cash Ledger (orders for business cards etc.), London, 1816-26, 1826-31; cash ledger, 1819-30; ledger, 1833-38; records book, 1836-41; case signature book, 1877-85; Richard Clay & Sons, London, ledger, 1888-92, 1892-1920; Richard Clay & Sons, Bungay, ledger, 1888-1916; mould and plate Books, 1905-15; list of plates, Oct 1887; Ledger, 'Standing Orders', Bungay, 1890s; works in progress (15 vols, 1897-1909); debenture registers 1888-1920; share records 1946-57; shareholders c1939-50; Joint Advisory

Council, charter and minutes 1944-57; pension books 1951-73; wages book, 1848-1913 (weekly rates by name, department, Christmas bonuses, annual totals); clerks and overseers wage books, 1914-35; directors' minutes, 1888-1961; general minute book 1918-25; minutes from meetings 1895; Bungay invoice books, 1988-53; sales daybooks, 1905-74; Richard Clay & Company, insurance salaries books, 1941-49; salaries books, 1965-68; cash books 1949-66; ledger, 1966-1971; accounts etc., 1968-1970; inventory and valuation 1933, 48 and 56; plans and related papers.

Records of Fletcher & Sons: memorandum and articles of association, 1898, 1956; minutes 1898-1959; debenture and share records 1898-1961; journals, daybooks and cash books; inventory and valuation 1956; salaries 1946-61; pension fund trust deeds 1958-63; reviews of books (MS and cuttings) 1844-1881.

See also: James Moran, *Clays of Bungay* (1984)

William Clowes Ltd, Beccles

The business was founded by William Clowes (1779-1847). Born in Chichester and apprenticed to a local printer, he moved to London in 1802 where he worked as a compositor. The following year his cousin, William Winchester, a stationer, lent him the money to set up a small business in Villiers Street. He mainly produced government forms for Winchester, but printed his first book in 1804. Three years later he moved to larger premises in Northumberland Court and by 1813 was dealing directly with several government departments. In 1823 Clowes installed the first steam-powered printing press to be used for the production of books on a commercial scale. He was appointed printer to the Royal Academy of Arts in 1824, and among other things, printed the *British Almanac* and *Penny Magazine* for the Society for the Diffusion of Useful Knowledge. Expansion continued prompting a further move to Duke Street, Blackfriars, in 1827. William's three sons, William II, George and Winchester, joined the firm in 1839 (it was restyled William Clowes & Sons), and by the following year, more than 600 were employed at Duke Street. Several major contracts were secured: the production and compilation of the catalogues for the 1851 Great Exhibition (including French and German editions), in 1865, the first issue of the *Law Reports* on behalf of the Council of Law Reporting, and in 1870, Charles Dicken's unfinished *The Mystery of Edwin Drood*, printed in fortnightly instalments.

The rapid growth of the printing industry in Scotland, where labour costs were lower,

The main composing room at William Clowes of Beccles.

began to threaten the viability of London printers, prompting a search for a suitable provincial business. In 1873, two young members of the family, W.C.K. Clowes and W.A. Clowes, purchased a small Beccles firm, the Caxton Press, previously owned by William Moore. Clowes & Clowes flourished, and by 1876 the value of the business had increased from £5,000 to £20,000, and the number of power-driven machines increased from four to fifteen. When in 1879 the second generation of the Clowes family retired, the two businesses were amalgamated and incorporated as a private limited company, William Clowes & Sons. Expansion continued at London: a code office to compile and supply secret codes to commercial firms for transmitting by cable was opened at Fenchurch Street; and to meet the demand for printing non-roman alphabets, Gilbert & Rimmington (established 1750) was purchased, bringing contracts from across the world. Following the First World War, Beccles concentrated on book-printing, with London specialising in the production of periodicals and general printing. In 1924 an advertising agency was opened which flourished until the Second World War. The Duke Street premises were destroyed in 1941. In 1946, Clowes was acquired by the family group, McCorquodale & Company, but retained its name and much of its independence. A programme of expansion followed, with the William Clowes & Sons Housing Society building a hundred houses by 1953 in order to attract labour to the town. During the 1960s and 1970s the main emphasis was on letter press and composing, the introduction of languages and mathematics for academic textbooks, and investment in training for keyboard skills. In 1983 the company entered the diaries market. Three years later,

McCorquodale was bought by Norton Opax, itself the target of an aggressive take-over by Bowater in 1989; in 1995 Bowater changed its name to Rexam plc. In July 1997 Clowes was the subject of a management buy-out. The company, which employs around 250, specialises in reference directory bespoke products (eg BA timetables - manipulating raw data, outputting in the form required and distributing). Diary production is in India, where labour costs are lower. The company is moving to a new factory at Ellough Industrial Estate, Beccles.

The great-great-grandson of the founder of William Clowes sitting on the biggest book in the world. Printed in 1930, it was part of a scheme to raise money for St Bartholomew's Hospital in London.

A few records are held by the company:

Ledger, Messrs Winchester & Son, 1811-18; inventory, Duke Street, London, 1879; Board Minutes, 1960; deeds of Beccles site.

The Caxton Magazine, vols 1 - 4, Sept 1927-1931

The company's museum houses a unique collection of composing, printing and binding machines and artefacts relating to the trade. Open daily 2-4 from June to September, admission is free. Enquiries to: Mr R Walding, William Clowes Ltd, Beccles, Suffolk, NR34 9QE.

See also: W.B. Clowes, *Family Business, 1803-1953* (1953)

W.S. Cowell Ltd, Ipswich

In 1818 Samuel Cowell set up as a printer and stationer at 10, Butter Market, Ipswich. Around 1826 further premises, together with an established tea, coffee, spice, and wine and spirit merchants business, were acquired in Market Lane. The tea business was carried on until the rebuilding of the Butter Market premises in 1893. Two years later, the purchase of the old Falcon Brewery enabled the expansion of the wine and spirit interests. A rag warehouse was also opened in 1885 as an ancillary to printing. By the end of the century, a wide range of printed goods and wholesale stationery (customised account books and paper bags etc) were supplied throughout the eastern counties and from the London sales office. In 1900 the works were extended and, soon after its invention, the monotype system of composing and type-casting was installed together with binding machinery enabling the production of high quality, illustrated catalogues. In 1936 the wholesale stationery section was reorganised and a new paper bag factory built. During the Second World War the company produced tombola (later bingo) tickets for the Admiralty, to supply entertainment for the Mediterranean fleet - a highly profitable venture which was continued after the war. A new factory was completed in 1950 and the old Market Lane works redeveloped as a finishing department. The next two decades saw an increasing variety of printing work: to supply educational and export markets; illustrated books and commercial brochures; and, from 1965, building society pass books and passports.

In 1954 a subsidiary company, Cowells Store Limited, was formed to handle the retail side of the business. An independent enterprise from 1963, it was sold to Wallace King Limited in 1970. The wine and spirit interests were also sold to John Harvey & Son, in 1959. In 1963 the printing business was acquired by the Glasgow based Grampian Holdings Limited. By the early 1980s, facing fierce foreign competition, it had become unprofitable and was sold to a second holding company. The town centre premises were sold in 1986. Three years later, following merger with Sans Serif Limited, the book and colour printing activities were discontinued. The bingo interests were disposed of in 1992.

Records deposited at SRO (I) HC 439:
The deposit is quite comprehensive and includes financial records 1874-1961 (accounts, balance sheets, ledgers); personnel (apprenticeships 1878-1930, wages, 1925-27); production; sales; premises and plant (plans, inventories, valuations 1872-1959); notes

on the history of the company; Athletic Club minutes, 1894-1942.

Green & Company, Crown Street, Lowestoft

Records deposited at SRO (L) Ac no 881:

Day book 1938-54; purchase ledger 1961-67; wages book 1961-71 (4 vols).

TEXTILES AND ALLIED INDUSTRIES

Arnold & Gould Ltd, Bells Lane, Glemsford
Horsehair manufacturers

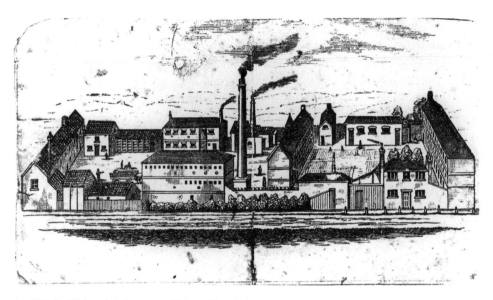

Arnold & Gould's horsehair factory at Bells Lane, Glemsford. The factory was first owned by H. Kolle & Son, who were established in 1848.

Arnold and Gould was founded in 1907 when Thomas Henry Gould acquired part of the horsehair factory owned by H. Kolle & Son at Bells Lane, Glemsford (established in 1848, the remainder of the factory was purchased in 1918-19). Gould had trained with a Mr Arnold, a well-known Liverpool horsehair dresser, who gave his name to the venture as a guarantee of quality. The firm imported raw horsehair, which was then processed in the factory and by outworkers, and sold to make brushes, violin bows, wigs and upholstery. At its peak it employed a workforce of around one hundred, many of them female. The company built up extensive export markets, especially in continental Europe: Germany, Bohemia, Czechoslovakia (sometimes and inexplicably listed separately) Austria, Holland. A flourishing trade with the USA after the Second World War collapsed in the mid-1970s when America sanctioned direct trade with China. After the death of Thomas Gould in 1945 the business continued to be run by his son, R.H.Gould. In 1979 it was sold to the present owner, Brian Whittaker.

Records deposited at SRO (B) HC 508:

Purchase details, showing invoices and suppliers (Chicago and Russia) 1928-1966; processing - detailed records of time and work done; sales - customers and credit rating, 1913-1935 and later; order books from November 1914 to 1920 and 1929-31; 1934, 1937/8, 1937-41 (including government orders); invoices for 1940; premises; staff - rates of pay, list of employees, 1939-44; income tax returns 1928-30; finance; administration; Long Melford Hair company (factory stock 1939-40); private correspondence of T.H.Gould. Few of the records refer to years earlier than the 1930s. Export and home sales are not listed separately; home sales predominated, especially from the 1930s. Some accounts and correspondence are held by the company.

Records at the Museum of East Anglian Life, Stowmarket:

76 D 44 Letter from Arnold and Gould; photographs.

A small collection of the company's objects is displayed in the Boby Building. Other objects are held in store (enquiries to the Curator).

See also records of the Hair Manufacturers Association, SRO (B) GC 514:

Minutes 1942-72; financial records 1942-72; correspondence 1958-72.

Firmin & Company, Ipswich
Sacking manufacturers

The business was founded in 1785 by Thomas Firmin at Fordham, near Colchester. His second son, George (1823-1907), moved to Ipswich in the mid-nineteenth century and set up in business. He opened a branch at Hadleigh in 1868-9. By the turn of the century Firmin's were making all kinds of canvas goods, weaving coconut matting, spinning their own twine and making their own rope, and developed a trade in house and garden furniture (for which they acquired Firmin's wood near Raydon as a source of timber). During the Great War the Ipswich factory expanded to make and mend nets and recondition sacks and bags and developed an extensive trade hiring sacks to farmers and merchants. In the 1920s and 1930s further branches were opened in Norwich, Peterborough and London. After the Second World War the Firmin Group of Companies was formed and diversification continued. In 1959 the old-established Ipswich firm of Rands & Jeckell, was acquired. Tents and marquees continued to be made, as well as hired out for shows, weddings etc. Hunter & Ford, a small power tool maker, was purchased in 1964 and expanded into a large unit supplying tools of all descriptions;

subsequently a sharpening workshop was opened. In 1986 the tent, marquee and hire departments were sold to Clyde Canvas of Ipswich and in August 1987 the remaining sections were taken over by MCP Building Supplies. The business retained the Firmin name, but family members formed a new tool and leisure hire company, Rite Hire Ltd. Late in 1989, when MCP's holding company went into liquidation, Firmin's was the subject of a management buyout. The new company, Firmins UK Ltd, retained the power tool, trailer and trailer accessories and sharpening operations and a manufacturing division making sacks, bags and tarpaulin covers. The company moved to new premises at Holywells Road, Ipswich, in September 1989.

Records deposited at SRO (I) HC435
Certificates and Royal Warrants of Appointment of Rands & Jeckell; correspondence of goods supplied to Royal Family 1911; maps, plans, drawings etc; photographs.
This is a small collection mainly relating to Rands & Jeckell.
See also files of newspaper cuttings.

Records held at the Museum of East Anglian Life, Stowmarket:
Copy of George Firmin's notebook, includes diagrams of tarpaulins and clothes, with customers names (c1860-70s).

The Gainsborough Silk Weaving Company Ltd, Sudbury
Weavers of furnishing fabrics

Reginald Warner, son of Metford Warner, proprietor of a well-known wallpaper manufacturing firm, Jeffries & Company, founded the company in 1903. He was first apprenticed to the English Silk Weaving Company at Ipswich and also studied weaving in Switzerland. When the Ipswich company went into liquidation, Warner set up on his own account with two second-hand looms in a cottage at Garden Place, Sudbury. The business expanded rapidly, moving to larger premises at Priory Walk in 1905. Two small properties were acquired shortly after the First World War. The business was incorporated as a private limited company in 1922 and two years later moved to its present factory in Alexandra Road. That year it made the wall fabrics and carpets for the Queen's dolls' house shown at the British Empire Exhibition. The fifty hand looms were mechanised during the 1930s, being powered by a steam boiler; electrification followed in the 1950s. These looms remain in use, but the first rapier looms were installed in the 1980s and electronic jacquards added in the 1990s.

Hand-loom weaving at the Gainsborough Silk Weaving Company, Sudbury, in the 1920s

The business remains in family hands and employs a workforce of around fifty. During the Second World War the market for high-class furnishings virtually disappeared; the firm lost 80 per cent of its staff but maintained production by manufacturing black out material. Otherwise it has continued to specialise in a wide range of high quality furnishing fabrics, including damasks, silk taffetas, tabourettes, brocatelles and satins, some woven on the early powered Jacquard looms. Its expertise in historical reproductions enables it to export fabrics to over thirty countries, many of which are supplied to national embassies and institutions such as the National Trust; the firm has also collaborated on reproduction of nineteenth-century furnishings for Windsor Castle. A range of wallpapers based on one of the founder's hand-painted designs was introduced in 1998.

Records held by the company (enquiries to the Company, Alexandra Road, Chilton, Sudbury, Suffolk, CO10 6XH):
Articles of Association; Directors' minutes; day books 1903-27 (2 vols); small ledgers (including stocks and orders) 1903-1930s (14 vols); ledger 1904-13; ledger ('bought book') 1903-18; bought day book 1918-34; bought ledgers (include weekly wage totals) 1907-71 (4 vols); trade ledger 1907; sales ledger 1913-26; private ledgers 1933-47 (include profit and loss accounts, 2 vols); private cash books 1922-50 (3 vols); cash books 1938-40, 1976-

78; dispatch books 1929-37 (9 vols); dispatch book sheets 1961; sample books 1928-49; balance sheets 1933-60; wages 1968-70s; sales 1981-84; photographs and newspaper cuttings.

Records of the English Silk Weaving Company, Ipswich: ledger 1898; day book 1898-1904; sample books 1896-1902.

The company has one of the largest private collections of archive fabrics in Britain, collected by the founder, mainly in France, Italy and Germany, in the early 1900s.

Glemsford Silk Mills Ltd, Glemsford
Silk throwsters and dyers

Glemsford Silk Mill was established at Chequers Lane, Glemsford, by Alexander Duff in 1824. By the 1840s around sixty workers were employed; thirty years later, more than 200. The mill was subsequently acquired by H.W. Eaton & Son, then, c1900, by Anderson & Robertson Ltd. In 1936 Glemsford Silk Mills Ltd became a subsidiary company of the Sudbury silk weavers, Stephen Walters & Sons Ltd. About that time electricity was brought into the mill to power some of the machines (although the water mill continued in use for some time). The mill was extended c1960 and shortly after the original building was demolished and replaced by a new mill. The company processes raw silk (imported in bales from China and Japan) into hanks for dyers; dyeing was added to the firm's activities in 1954. The silk is destined for a wide variety of uses: furnishing fabrics, church and academic regalia, tie fabrics, handkerchiefs, threads for lace making and embroidery and dress fabrics, including the Queen's coronation robe, Prince Charles' investiture gown and the wedding dresses of Princess Anne and Lady Diana Spencer. The company continues to trade.

Records deposited at SRO (B) HC 525
The records are not extensive. They include plans and correspondence; buildings; processes; others - miscellaneous.

See also: Sir Frank Warner. *The Silk industry of the UK* (Dawes, London, n.d. c1902)

D. Gurteen & Sons Ltd, Chauntry Mill, Haverhill
Clothing manufacturers

The factory floor at Gurteens, c1881

The business was founded c1784 by Daniel Gurteen, a merchant and weaver of fustians and checks. By 1819 the company was also selling ready-to-wear smocks. In 1831 approximately 300 out-workers were employed as spinners and weavers. The introduction of steam power in 1856 for weaving and subsequently to power sewing machines enabled the shift to factory production and the manufacture of ready made clothing for the growing mass market. After 1870 the firm diversified into the manufacture of leather workwear for agricultural workers, and expanded the weaving operation to produce huckaback towelling and horsehair fabrics for the tailoring, millinery and corsetry trades. A dyehouse was also installed to enable the company to dye its own woven drabbetts and a unit for dressing horsehair. In the 1880s a department making rag rugs was established to give work to unemployed local mat-makers; it grew to employ 250 weavers. By the late 1880s, D. Gurteen & Sons, employing almost 4,000 workers, had become one of the largest clothing manufacturers in the country, with extensive national and overseas markets.

Almost a century later: Gurteens in the 1970s

During the 1914-18 war the company contracted for army uniforms and continued to make inexpensive menswear and to export work clothes, especially to the colonies. A small group of retail shops in Cambridgeshire and Lincolnshire was acquired. The focus on the utility, heavyweight and industrial areas of the market persisted throughout the inter-war years but changed conditions after the Second World War forced a period of adaptation. Several older departments were closed and the emphasis shifted away from heavy industrial clothing to modern lightweight menswear. Faced with growing competition for local labour, new factories with up-to-date technology were opened at Hadleigh (1961) and Ely (1964). From 1972 production concentrated exclusively on men's lightweight jackets and casual trousers, but despite these innovations, Gurteens faced the growing problem of cheap imports from developing countries. In response, the company began marketing imported ready-made garments, but in order to compete, all manufacturing was moved out of Britain in the mid-1990s. The business was registered as a private limited company in 1929 and remains in family hands.

Records held by the company (enquiries to D. Gurteen & Sons Ltd, Chauntry Mills, Haverhill, Suffolk, CB9 8AZ; email: sales@gurteen.co.uk):

Directors' minutes, from 1917 (7 vols); constitution and rules 1950s-77; day books 1784-1825, 1900-58 (7 vols); ledgers 1885-1974 (13 vols); journals 1892-1915, 1950s, 1972 (4 vols); cash accounts 1870-1924; analysis book 1885-99; memoranda of costings 1884-49; misc accounting records 1927-60; order books 1893-1951, 1893-c1971 (19 vols); sales ledgers, 1900s-1964 (6 vols); area sales analysis books 1928-60s (5 vols); customer address and index books c1908-40 (2 vols); despatch book c1911-17; shipping book 1911-21; stock books 1893-1951 (3 vols); stock lists 1915-17; making accounts 1892-98, 1914-54 (4 vols); production notebook c1863; factory diaries 1889-c1911 (3 vols); pattern and sample books 1912-13, 1922-42 (6 vols); salaries book 1889; salaries, wages and staff records, mainly 1931-59 (26 vols); deeds 17-20th century; gurteen family financial, property and misc papers 19-20th century; trade catalogues, design cards, circulars and other printed material 19-20 century.

The company also has a small museum which is open by appointment.

See also: *Guide*, 8 (950)
Sara Payne, *The Gurteens of Haverhill: Two Hundred Years of Suffolk Textiles* (1984)

Gurteen's hair weaving factory, c1900

Haverhill Rope, Twine and Sack Company

The Haverhill Rope, Twine & Sack Company: 'strand laying' – attaching the strands to the 'traveller'.

The business of James Henderson & Company of Burton End, Haverhill, is listed in trade directories by 1888 but was probably formed some time before this. It appears to have been owned by a Leeds firm, Boils. It was subsequently acquired by Bertram L. Radford, William Whiting and a Mr Argent and restyled the Haverhill Rope, Twine and Sack Company (later the Haverhill Rope Company Ltd). Argent was quickly bought out by the remaining partners who continued until the deed expired in 1927. Radford then went into partnership with his son-in-law, Tom Farr.

The company made rope, twine, stack, wagon and drum cloths and made and hired out marquees and tents. Hemp and jute were imported from several countries; one long-running contract was for jute washing lines which were exported to South Africa. Old hawsers were also bought from the admiralty; these were unwound, then the inner core tarred and re-used. A survey of rural industries conducted in 1923 noted that ropes were still hand-made. After the First World War, a new rope walk was constructed from ex-army huts. Power driven machinery was installed and rope making ceased at the old rope walk in 1921. The machinery was designed to work soft rope-making fibres (cotton, hemp and jute), but with the growing popularity of sisal (a hard fibre) rope, it became cheaper to buy rope ready-made and concentrate on selling. One spinner and ropemaker was employed as an out-worker to make small fishing nets. By the 1940s the firm was also making customised lorry aprons and covers. The business appears to have closed in the 1970s.

Records held by Haverhill and District Local History Society:
Day Books 1919-73 (39 vols); cash book 1942-46; day books, orders for customised sacks, lorry covers and tarpaulins (with drawings) 1948-72 (13 vols).
Enquiries to: Local History Centre, Town Hall Arts Centre, High Street, Haverhill, Suffolk.

A display of the company's machinery and objects is housed in the Boby Building, the Museum of East Anglian Life, Stowmarket.

See also: E.J. Yaxley, 'A Suffolk Rope-Walk', *East Anglian Magazine*, August 1967.

Phillips & Piper Ltd, Old Foundry Lane, Ipswich
Clothing manufacturers

In 1858 Thomas Phillips of Ipswich went into partnership with Charles Ingram, originally from Stourpaine, Dorset, to trade as Phillips & Ingram, drapers and woollen merchants, at the Old Butter Market, Ipswich. By the 1860s the business had changed its name to Phillips & Piper. It subsequently opened branches at Jevens Street, London, and at Bristol. In 1900 it was incorporated as a private limited company, merging with another Ipswich firm, the London & East Anglian Tailoring Company. The business expanded rapidly, specialising in high quality menswear and riding clothes; the latter were sold under the Foxley label and supplied to Harrods and the American market. In 1903 the Christchurch Clothing Works in Old Foundry Road were opened and a manufacturing department added to the Bristol branch.

The firm continued to be run by the Phillips family for four generations. In the 1970s it was hit by changing fashions and cheap imports and then by the recession after 1979. Unable to shift downmarket easily, the firm closed in 1982 after heavy losses with the loss of 190 jobs. Two well-known brand names, Pytchley and Belvoir, were sold to Austin Reed who formed a new company, Phillips & Piper Country Clothing, trading at Thirsk. Subsequently two ex-directors re-purchased the Lambourne label and opened a new company at Ipswich, Merage Clothing Company, making as before men's quality clothing and riding gear.

Records deposited at SRO(I) HC414:

Minutes etc, no public access for 30 years from latest date each item; wages records, employee's registers, accident register and clinic registers, no public access for 75 years from latest date each item.

Partnership agreement, Phillips & Ingram, 1859; prospectus, 1900; memoranda of association, 1900 and 1951; minutes: board and annual general meeting minute books, 1900-1977; minutes of advisory committee on production; accounts: balance sheets and profit and loss accounts, 1863-1910; balance sheets and annual accounts, 1889-1922; printed reports and balance sheets, 1901-81; rough annual accounts, 1902-1910; cash books, 1863-1939; monthly returns, 1900-23; stocktaking accounts, 1901-1923; summary of abstracts of accounts, 1905-20; trading accounts, 1945-48; balance sheet and trading accounts, 1900, 1912-25; register of members, share ledgers, debentures, 1900-73; annual returns of members, 1909-54; share certificates, 1920-80; resolutions re capital recommendations, 1920-22; wages accounts, 1901-65; dividend and interest account, 1911-65; summary of account: sales, credits, manufacturing returns and purchases, 1933-59; sales accounts, 1924-54; monthly sales account (small notebook), 1855-91; accounts of sales, returns, liabilities, c1870-98; monthly and yearly returns, 1855-99; manufacturers returns, 1931-35; foreign woollen day book, No.7, 1934-42; foreign sales day book, No.6, 1931-35; account of cash creditors (Piper family), 1893-94; bad debts written off, 1914-38, 1940-66; Scotch, Irish and foreign bad debts, 1930-50; miscellaneous unsorted items, 1916-30.

Records of the London & East Anglian Tailoring Company (formerly Manufacturing Company):

Annual accounts, 1890-99; balance sheet, 1899; lease of parts of warehouse, 17, Union Street, City of London; guard books and trade lists, 1931-57; guard books and advertisements, 1950-60; guard books, editorial and newspaper press-cuttings and illustrations, 1931-66; plans and drawings, unsorted.

William Pretty & Sons, Ipswich
Corset and lingerie manufacturers

William Pretty & Sons corset factory, built at Tower Ramparts, Ipswich, in 1881, and extended in the 1930s. The factory was closed in 1982 and demolished the following year.

The business grew out of the linen and silk mercers shop opened by Robert Footman at the Butter Market, Ipswich, in 1815. After his death in 1824 his brother John added a woollen drapery department and moved to larger premises on Cornhill. William Pretty, the son of a Bacton tailor and draper, joined the business in 1934. It moved again to nearby Westgate Street in 1842 and in 1858 the first corset factory was built behind the shop in Silent Street. A.F. Nicolson, another Ipswich draper, and William Pretty subsequently became partners in the firm which was restyled Footman, Pretty & Nicolson (later Footman Pretty & Company). The shop and stay factory became separate businesses, with William Pretty developing the latter; when he died in 1889, his son, William, became sole proprietor. In 1881-2 a new factory, fitted with American machinery, was built at Tower Ramparts. Branches were opened at Bury St Edmunds, Sudbury, Hadleigh, Stowmarket, Beccles, Diss and King's Lynn; the initial manufacturing processes were completed at the branches and the garments finished at Ipswich. By the turn of the century the firm employed around 1,200 hands, almost half at Ipswich, and a further 300 outworkers. In 1904 a crèche with trained nurses was set up to care for the workers' children; other welfare measures, such as a blanket club and soup kitchen, were also provided.

William Pretty II died in 1916 and the fortunes of the business declined significantly thereafter with the workforce falling to around 350. In 1930 the company was acquired by R.& W.H. Symington & Company Ltd of Market Harborough, registered as a private limited company and re-named William Pretty & Sons (1930) Ltd. Its fortunes were restored mainly through diversification into large-scale production of artificial silk underwear which put the company at the forefront of the world market. Between 1930 and 1938 production increased from 500 dozen garments a week to 1,000 dozen a day. A four-storey extension was added to accommodate extra staff, and by 1938 the workforce had again increased to 1,300. During the Second World War many of the company's wholesale customers ceased trading but subsequently Prettys supplied catalogue companies such as Littlewoods, besides such major retailers as Marks & Spencer and British Home Stores. The company was acquired by Courtaulds in 1968. In the following decade the range of products was extended to include maternity wear, swimwear and children's clothes. The factory was closed in 1982 and the building partly demolished the following year. Courtaulds opened a new factory under the name of Rowley on the Hadleigh Road Estate making maternity wear, children's clothes and school uniforms, producing own-label goods. The factory continues to trade.
Most of the company's records have been destroyed.

Records deposited at SRO (I) HD 1651/2
Commemorative brochure 1820-1938; photographs, including 1858 stay factory, 1881 corset factory, factory crèche 1904. See also newspaper cuttings.

Records deposited at Leicester Record Office (included in the R.&.W.H. Symington archive): DE 2262

Letters relating to the takeover of William Pretty & Company, 1930; plan of the factory.

Records held by Rowley, Ipswich: Patents from the 1870s.

A collection of photographs and tape recordings of Pretty's employees is held by the Ipswich Women's History Group. Enquiries to Miss Jenny Smith (01473 740041) or Mrs Dee Crowe (01473 253917).

See also: 'A short history of Footmans' (typescript), held by the Business Archive Council, ref 656 Foo.

The corset stitching room at William Pretty & Sons, c1930.

William Rought Ltd, Brandon
Hatters' furriers

The business of preparing rabbit and hare skins for hatters reputedly started c1790. William Rought was born in 1818. (His father Judd had married into the family of a furrier, Malt, in 1805.) He had one daughter, whose married name was Witta. Her son took over the business in c1890 and changed his name to Rought to suit his grandfather's wishes, apparently by adding 'Rought' to his own name. By the 1870s the business employed 160 women in preparing and cutting rabbit and hare skins for making hats and felts for the clothiers in Yorkshire. It was incorporated as a private limited company in 1924 to carry on the business of Albert Rought Rought (sic). It became one of the chief centres of this branch of the furrier trade, employing nearly 500 at the peak. Much of the product was exported. The business declined with changing tastes in fashion but the real death knell came with the advent of myxomatosis and the firm closed in 1967.

Records deposted at SRO (B) HC 521

Memoranda and articles of association, 1924, letter book c1883-5, profits and loss and capital a/c, 1902-16, private ledgers (3) 1924-39, 1949-50, ledgers (5) 1891, 1900-13. day books (5) 1865-71, 1904-33, 1947-74, journals (4) 1913-60, cash books (7) 1919-26, 1932-65, bank books (2) 1927-37, personal expense a/c books 1907-13, receipt and payment a/c books (4) 1900-19, bought and sold ledgers (7) 1913-59, invoices (8 vols) 1904-59, notes re skins bought 1884-1913, price lists 1902-3, stock books 1894, work book 1937-44, wages books (3) 1917-31, with lists of employees; family and estate papers 1838-1906 inc letter books (3) 1909-24, photographs c1920.

Some of the records are held off site and need 48 hours notice.

See also: *Guides* vol. 8

The Rural Industries of England and Wales, Vol II (OUP, 1926), p.122

A.D.Bayne, *Royal Illustrated History of Eastern England,* Vol 1 (1872).

W. & A.J. Turner Ltd, Ipswich
Tanners

The firm originally dates from 1716 in Ipswich. Through the nineteenth century production was based in Bures; early in the twentieth century works were opened in Bramford Road, Ipswich. It was taken over by Allied Leather Industries 1972 and closed 1987. By the time of its closure it had come to specialise in heavy leather tanning.

Redcords deposited at SRO (I) HC 452:

Hides processed 1930-5, 1935-51; stock book 1938-45; harness leather 1930-7

At the Museum of Leathercraft, Northampton:

Preparing rabbit skins at William Rought Ltd, the Brandon hatters' furriers.

Directors minute book, 1937-54, letter book 1904-1913, account books (3) 1912-70, ledger 1923-33, private journals 1930s, notebook on bends ordered and delivered 1930s, contracts 1950s and 1980s, price lists 1924-39, catalogue 1932-3.

See also: *Guide*, vol. 8 (1184)

H. Underwood and Sons Ltd, Ipswich
Leather and footwear manufacturers

Founded in 1870 by Henry Underwood at 40, Upper Brook Street, Ipswich, in 1969 the business moved to the Hadleigh Road Industrial Estate, then in 1988 to Whitehouse Industrial Estate. Initially the firm manufactured leather goods and footwear, retailing these products besides hardware and cycles. Subsequently it became a wholesale distributor of footwear.

Records deposited at SRO (I) HC 445:
Company agreements, 1897; Financial and trading records, from 1908; purchase records, from 1878; photographs.

Vanners, Sudbury
Silk weavers

The business, based at Spitalfields, London, was founded c1829 by John Vanner (1800-1866), a silk weaver and merchant of Huguenot origin. The firm initially produced high quality silks and brocades, but by the 1851 Great Exhibition, was specialising in silk for umbrellas and parasols. The weaving of umbrella silk formed the basis for expansion in the second half of the nineteenth century, the firm virtually holding the monopoly of production for many years. In 1871 a warehouse at Glemsford, Suffolk, was rented to serve the hand-loom weavers employed by the company; a second was opened at Haverhill three years later. The headquarters of the business remained in London, but by 1886 the two Suffolk factories employed 400-500 workers. Faced with increasing competition from French weavers and the introduction of power looms, by the end of the century employment had fallen by nearly half, and in 1900 J.Vanner & Sons was sold to George and Frank Fennell, who had recently installed power looms at their factory at Girling Road, Sudbury. The company was renamed Vanners & Fennell Brothers. The Glemsford property was sold five years later.

After the First World War the firm diversified into weaving silk for cravats and neckties, and by 1938 this had superseded umbrella silk as the mainstay of production. Tailoring silks were added in the early 1930s. The Sudbury Silk Weaving Company was purchased in 1924 bringing valuable managerial talent; the Gregory Street property was extended in 1928 and again in 1934. After the Second World War throwing and dyeing plants were built at Girling Street to reduce dependence upon north of England suppliers. In 1958 more than 80 per cent of the Jacquard looms were producing silk for 'crested clubs': regimental, club and old school ties. By the early 1970s only one loom was weaving umbrella silk, another, tailoring silks. In 1968, following several offers from larger firms, Vanners merged with David Evans & Company of Crayford, a leading specialist in silk printing (a possibility first discussed in 1951). David Evans, Vanners & Company was bought by Sekers International for £1.6 million in 1980. Sekers was subsequently acquired by Stoddard Holdings Plc, a carpet manufacturer based in Scotland and in February 1989 Vanners became the subject of a management buy-out. The company is still trading.

Records held by:
Midland Bank plc: enquires to Midland Bank Group Archives

Private ledgers 1854-95; private journals 1840-1900; cash books 1858-74, 1892-1906; cash and ledgers 1874-86; bought ledger 1865-80; summary of goods, private, cash and bought ledgers 1896-1900; Vanner family accounts; diaries and other papers (45 vols) 1839-1909.

Victoria and Albert Museum: enquires to Department of Textile Furnishings and Dress Pattern books c1700-30, 1820-6 in private collection.

Records deposited at SRO (B) HC 553:

Vanners & Fennell Bros Ltd, order book, 1910-24; specification book for silks (with patterns) 1914-19; ledger 1864-65; summary production records 1900-64, c1917; printed material on the history of the silk industry (twentieth century).

See also: *Guide,* vol. 8, 738

Stanley Chapman, 'Vanners in the English Silk Industry' *Textile History*, 23 (1), 1992, pp.71-86.

Webb & Son (Combs) Ltd, Stowmarket
Tanners

In 1711 Thomas Denny was given £100 by his father to sink a tanyard at Combs, near Stowmarket. This remained in Denny family hands until 1776 when it was leased to an employee, Joseph Antrim Webb (d1809). By a series of mortgages the Webb family increased their interest and they acquired the tannery outright in 1843. Growth in production was encouraged by repeal of the leather duties in 1830, and the numbers employed increased from fewer than fifty in the 1830s to 250 in the 1880s. By the late nineteenth century the firm had become well known for its machine belts made from cow hides. The Webb family also bought up smallholdings and in 1865 built a Model Farm where they pioneered agricultural innovations; the farm later became a limited company. The tannery was run by the family as a series of partnerships until it was registered as a limited company in 1911. When Joseph Vertue Webb died in 1908 it passed to his sister's family, the Portways, in whose ownership it remained. After the Second World War production was increasingly mechanised, and in 1958 the old tanning processes were discontinued in favour of sueded shearling production, processing sheepskins from all over the world, and employing 150 people in the mid 1980s. However, mild winters reduced demand for this product and production ceased in

The tanners, Webb & Sons, were renowned in the nineteenth century for the manufacture of leather machine belts from cowhides. This picture shows stacks of oak-tree bark at the Bark Yards, Combs Tannery, c1900.

September 1988. The company is still operational and owns the tannery which has been converted into mini-industrial units.

The records are the most important collection of tanning records; the earliest dated records are for 1774, with partnership records from 1809.

Records held by the company - enquiries to N. W. Porthway:
Dissolution of partnership 1848, partnership a/c and ledger 1809-17, executorship letters and papers 1864-81, transfers and balances 1916-45, letter books (63) 1841-7, 1898-1911, 1930s, ledgers (26) 1848-1964, journals (8) 1776-1944, day books (25) 1839-1936, cash books (42) 1849-1971, a/c books (11) 1818-1904, 1935-65, bank books (25) 1830s-1930, purchase and sales books (16) 1927-60, factors consignments 1911-39 John Haywood in a/c for sheep, 1875-87, Stowmarket shop ledgers and stock book 1855-1901, agreements and contracts 1847-99, receipts orders etc., 1925-1950, details of other firms, 1866-84, 1909-12, warehouse or despatch books 1877-1940, stock books and ledgers 1817-1947, bark books 1885-1943, works diary 1834-8, a/c book for piece work 1829-47, fleece wool record 1861-1912, scale book 1933-4, trial, recipe and test books, 1830, 1851-65, 1940-1957, inventory and memo books 1830s- 1896, work a/c books, curriers books, early 20th C.,

wages books (47 vols) 1848-1968, valuations books, insurance policies, 20th C maps etc., leather tax papers, 1774-1818, govt. controls and returns 1939-45, Leather Belting Federation corresp. 1940s , model farm a/c, stock and wages records, valuations (52 vols) 1823-20th C, family personal property and local authority society papers 19th-20th C; collection of photographs.

See *Guide*, vol. 8, 1191

A small collection of objects is displayed in the Boby Building at the Museum of East Anglian Life, Stowmarket.

MISCELLANEOUS

Brandon Gun Flint Company

Flint knapping and the production of flint locks, one of the oldest British industries, was practised at Brandon for several centuries. The quality of the flints at Long Heath was said to equal any to be found worldwide, and during the Napoleonic Wars the demand was such that the majority of the local population were employed in production. In 1835 flint locks were superseded by percussion caps and the industry declined considerably. To encourage its revival, the Brandon Gun Flint Company (with 138 shares of £25) was formed three years later. Flints were exported throughout the world and, by 1868, thirty-six flint knappers were employed. A decade later the numbers had fallen to twenty-six. The demand for old fashioned fire-arms from West Africa and the Gold Coast sustained the industry into the twentieth century, but by 1923 only four flint knappers remained at work.

Records deposited at SRO (B) HC 506
Shares, deeds, memo book 1837-8; work books 1837-48; letter books, ledgers, minute books, stock and account books.

See also: *The Rural Industries of England and Wales*, Vol III, Survey on behalf of the Agricultural Economics Research Institute, Oxford (1927).

Churchmans Ltd, Ipswich
Cigarette and cigar manufacturers

The business, founded in 1790, began as a small pipe tobacco manufacturer and shop at Hyde Park Corner, Ipswich. In 1888, William Alfred and Arthur Charles Churchman, grandsons of the founder, succeeded their father, Henry, in the business. At that time output was mainly shag, snuff and tobacco. By 1890 the company was also making 'white cigarettes' and six years later installed one of the first cigarette making machines, producing 20,000 cigarettes an hour; the famous 'Churchman's No1' brand dates from this period. The following year a new factory was opened in Portman Road. In 1902 W.A. & A.C. Churchman Ltd joined the Imperial Tobacco Company (of Great Britain and Ireland) Ltd, formed the previous year in response to the American invasion of the British cigarette market.

The factory was extended several times during the inter-war years. In 1961 W.A. & A.C. Churchman amalgamated with Lambert & Butler and Edwards, Ringer & Bigg, becoming Churchman, Lambert & Ringer; the company was renamed Churchmans in 1965. By this time production was concentrated on cigars, and the following August, Churchmans acquired Herbert Merchant, the main UK agents for Henri Wintermans, the Dutch cigar manufacturers. With a workforce of over 1,000, the factory produced in excess of one million cigars a day. In 1972 the company ceased to be a separate brand of Imperial Tobacco Company; the cigar business was integrated with John Player & Sons, the tobacco interests with Ogdens of Liverpool. In May 1992, in order to streamline operations, the parent company moved all production to Bristol. Churchmans closed with the loss of over 400 jobs.

Records deposited at SRO (I) HC 446
Prime cost records, 1907-39; comparative returns on sales, 1915-39; trademark registers, 1908-62; wages, 1918-42; photographs. Also a file on employees who were killed in the forces, 1940-49 – this is confidential until 2025.

Felixstowe Dock & Railway Company
Transport and communication

The business, initially known as the Felixstowe Railway and Pier Company, was founded in 1875 by George Tomline of Orwell Park, Nacton, one of the largest landowners in Suffolk. A railway line, linking Felixstowe through a junction with the Great Eastern Railway at Westerfield, to Ipswich, was opened in 1877. Two years later an agreement was made for the GER to operate the railway and pier and the name of the business was changed to the Felixstowe Railway and Dock Company; this was subsequently reversed to Felixstowe Dock and Railway Company to reflect its main interest. Excavation of the dock began in 1881 and, after several setbacks, the first steamer arrived in 1886. Attempts to attract industry were hampered by the GER who developed rail links at Ipswich Dock and its own steamer terminal at Parkeston Quay, Harwich, but trade was slowly built up in timber, roadstone and malt. A north quay was completed in 1906 and the following year the Colchester milling firm of E. Marriage & Son Ltd built the East Anglian Mills, bringing increasing imports of wheat and exports of flour. The port was involved in war work in 1914-18 and during the Second World War was occupied by the Royal Navy and Airforce, with part of the premises requisitioned as a supply depot. Consequently by the late 1940s it was run down, had poor facilities, and appeared to have little future.

In 1951 the port was bought by H. Gordon Parker for £50,000. The company obtained approval for handling government explosives and military stores and began to build up trade in tank storage of bulk liquids, particularly chemical solvents for the growing plastics industry. In 1961 a subsidiary company, Felixstowe Tank Developments Ltd, was formed to handle these interests (a controlling interest was sold in 1975 to Tankfreight Ltd). The company also pioneered several new cargo handling techniques (in 1956 Felixstowe was the first port in England to use pallets and fork lift trucks) and much new equipment was designed and built internally. A port development consultancy service was established which advised ports in the Middle East, India and many other parts of the world. In the decade 1964-73 the total tonnage of cargo handled rose almost tenfold to 3,463,425 tonnes. A major factor in this rapid expansion was the relative freedom from strikes and demarcation practices, higher labour productivity in comparison with other major ports, and the willing acceptance of new techniques. Roll-on, roll-off services were developed from the mid-1960s, with a purpose-built passenger terminal added in 1975. The first container terminal was completed in 1968.

In October 1975 British Transport Docks made a £5¼ million offer for the company, but the following February a successful counter-bid was made by European Ferries Ltd. Continued investment ensured the rate of expansion continued. In 1977, container handling capacity was increased by 60 per cent and the most advanced equipment installed. With the opening of the Dooley and Walton Terminals in 1981 Felixstowe became the leading UK container port. Road improvements and the opening of the Orwell Road Bridge in 1982, the completion of a new deep-water channel approach in 1985 and the opening of the Trinity Container Terminal the following year placed Felixstowe among the world's top twenty ports. The company is now part of the Hutchison group.

Records deposited at SRO (I) HC 402:
Directors Minutes 1875-1921 and 1944-74; minutes of Committees 1961-72, Orwell Ballast; financial: registers of shares and debentures, 1877-1965; same for Orwell Ballast; same for Felixstowe Dock and Estates; same for Grain Silos; agreements, conveyances, miscellaneous from 1879.

There is a further deposit made by Mr T.L. Savage former company secretary [in class list but not fully catalogued]. These are very extensive. They include Directors minute books, 1921-43; share registers 1875-1966; detailed financial records including account books to the 1960s; letter books, Dock copies, 1886-1940, private copy, 1931-1947.

See also: Robert Malster, *Felixstowe, 1886-1986: 100 Years a Working Port* (Port of Felixstowe, 1986)

John George & Sons Ltd. Welnetham, Bury St Edmunds
Hand tool makers

John George and Sons Ltd was a London based firm of hardware factors which decided to move into manufacturing wooden hand tools in 1911. They had hitherto bought such tools as wooden hay rakes and parts for scythes and other tools from local makers and it was one such, A.G. Last, who persuaded Stanley George to take over his business and build a factory in Welnetham. The works were opened in 1912 and coppice woods nearby in Felsham Hall woods were leased to provide a steady supply of ash, birch, alder, hazel and willow. As well as rakes and scythe sneaths a variety of other tools and artefacts were produced - handles, pegs, sheep hurdles, stable forks. A further 300 acres of woodland were bought in 1934 to meet growing demand. Following a fire in 1939, which unfortunately destroyed many early records, the works were substantially re-built. A decline in trade in the 1960s resulted in the Welnetham works going into liquidation in 1967. In 1970 the business was bought by the Litchfield family, with the firm trading as Welnetham Woodwork Ltd. The woodland was bought by the Society for the Preservation of Nature Reserves to become Bradfield Hall Nature Reserve. The firm changed hands again in 1974 and finally in 1984 when bought by a furniture designer and maker.

Records deposited in the Rural History Centre and Museum of Rural Life, University of Reading:
Legal records, correspondence 1943, 1949, tenancy agreement 1965; accounts, 1949-1970, wages accounts books 1937-1943 and 1963-4; invoice books, 1938-1970, 1978, credits book 1917-43, invoice files 1962-4, banking records 1963-70 and accounting papers 1961-7; factory records, registers as required under various factory acts; labour records, 1942-54 as made for Ministry of Labour and National Service, income tax and N.I., 1963-71, wage rates and hours of work 1963-7, illness 1965-9; production records, 1954-9, 1959-66, census of production returns 1948, 1951, stock records 1951-63, 1963-7, despatch records 1927-49, 1948-63, 1970-3, 1975-8; order records, 1965-7, for Ministry of Works 1949-56, Min of Supply 1950-3, British Railways 1954, correspondence 1950-1; sales records, annual summaries 1956-66, cards relating to individual sales, various from 1948-51; materials - correspondence relating to purchase of timber from various suppliers, 1943-66, with Ministry of Supply 1942-50, metal files and rasps, 1941-50, goods received 1951-

69; buildings and plant records, various concerning purchases and insurance 1951 to 1970; woods records, annual cutting 1936-65 and felling plans 1936-60, various concerning sales 1948-59, 1950-62, hunting and shooting rights in Felsham Hall 1933 to 1966, rabbit clearance 1956- 64 and woods maintenance 1940-2, 1049-50, 1959, 1955-6; general correspondence, letter books 1938-67; publicity and advertising records, trade literature and price lists 1970, 1971, 1974, 1975, publicity records 1950s, labels and tags, advertising and retail prices 1955-6.

Ipswich Port Authority
Transport and communication

Ipswich has been a port since at least the 13th century - a Collector of Customs was appointed in 1280. In later years it suffered a decline both because of the silting of the river, coupled with the increase in size of ships, which hindered navigation and a decline in the industrial activity of its hinterland. However, a revival in trade was evident from the mid-eighteenth century. Once again silting of the river presented navigation problems and various acts of parliament were passed to allow dredging, widening and other improvements. In 1805 the River Commissioners undertook improvements to the river; in 1837 work began on building a dock. This marked the beginnings of the Dock Commissioners' responsibility. Railway links were intalled in 1846-49 and further expansion followed with the introduction of steam powered vessels. In turn these demanded yet deeper dredging and a deep water berth was opened in Butterman's Bay. In 1897 a swing bridge was opened to link different parts of the port area. Expansion and improvements continued with the installation of specialised facilities such as those for grain handling. After the Second World War special provision was made for the bulk handling of chemicals - thought to be the first of any British port. Further adaptations continued in the post-war years as demand grew. In 1969 roll-on roll-off facilities were made for commercial transport. In 1982 a grain shipping terminal was opened at Cliff Quay and two years later a £2.75 million container terminal. By 1989 the port was the leading short-sea container port in the UK, ranking fourth for worldwide container trade, handling annual traffic of 5 million tons. The port became part of Associated British Ports in 1997.

Records deposited at SRO (I) EL1

These records have a full and detailed catalogue prepared by the Historical Manuscripts Division for SRO in 1984, (viii + 186pp.). This is a brief summary.

Formal minutes of the Orwell River Comissioners, 1805-1837 and of the Dock Commissioners, 1837-1945; extensive correspondence on the period from construction of the dock to the twentieth century; maps, plans and drawings from 1790s; reports, letter books, financial records, property deeds; local papers; contract papers, pilotage, navigation and dredging records; parliamentary papers relating to numerous Acts of Parliament; Railways and Tramways, sewage disposal; miscellanea.

Harry Rumsby and Sons, Bungay
Iron and brass founders, manufacturers of stoves and agricultural implements

Records deposited at SRO (I) HC 406/2:
Ledgers (8) 1819-33, 1887-1901, 1903-4, daybooks (2) 1923-45

An advert for Gurteen's breeches from their 'Fit and Strong' range of work-wear, c.1930